DEPRESSION

ADVANCE READING COPY

Defeating Depression: Run It Away!

John Stewart

ISBN: 0-9444-10-4
$11.95, 120 pp., Exceptional Books

Publicity/Keeler Communication/505-466-4040

Defeating

DEPRESSION

Run It away!

by

John Stewart

First Edition
Manufactured in the United States of America

Editors: Mary Mann and Beverly Talley
Cover and book design: John Cole, GRAPHIC DESIGNER
Cover photograph: Len Kaltman
Model: Carolyn Smith

ISBN 0–944482–10–4

Library of Congress Catalog Card Number 94–61292

EXCEPTIONAL BOOKS, LTD.
798 47th Street
Los Alamos, New Mexico 87544
(505) 662-6601

1 2 3 4 5 6 7 8 9 10

CONTENTS

PREFACE

This little book was written to convince those who suffer from depression that physical activity is often a cure for the symptoms of depression. Next is the task of convincing these same people that they should try physical activity because it will work for them. The final task is to convince them to stay with a physical activity program to prevent the recurrence of depression.

My goal was to condense the information I acquired from extensive reading in both the popular and professional media and from personal experience into a small volume that could be read in one afternoon or even during two lunch hours. The saga of my battle with depression and my final victory over it could easily be presented in such limited space, but would everyone be convinced by the story? More convincing might be a reprint of most of the articles and books detailing relevant scientific experiments and case studies, describing exercise-induced psychological changes, and presenting theories on the positive mood changes induced by physical activity—but the reprint volume would be thousands of pages long. Few of us have enough lunch hours available to read all the material I examined to learn why my solution to depression worked. Interviews with those therapists who actually exercise with their depressed patients because of their strong belief that physical activity is a better and faster cure than other prescriptions they have available would also be convincing. Again, space and time were my limiting factors.

Like the television evangelist, I want as many converts as possible; therefore, I have presented a smattering of all convincing arguments. My experience is described, scientific studies are presented, and hypotheses and theories are mentioned. But *Defeating Depression* can be read in two lunch hours—perhaps the remainder of your lunch hours will go toward your own efforts to use what you read here to defeat your own depression.

Many excellent and scholarly works have been published on exercise-induced positive mood changes. These works are, for the most part, addressed to the mental health practitioner or the scientist; most present convincing evidence that physical activity will alleviate depression. Unfortunately, these works devote little or no space to convincing those who suffer from depression to try exercise as a possible cure. My thinking is that the person who suffers from depression is the person who needs to know the most about this therapy and how to use it; therefore, *Defeating Depression* addresses primarily that person. I truly hope that my arguments are convincing and that a majority of my readers will try this self-administered treatment.

Most salesmanship courses teach that product information needs to be well-founded, factual, and concise. It is well known that once the product information is perfected and the initial presentation is made to the potential customer, several shorter follow-up presentations will be required to complete the sale. The person suffering from depression is my potential customer. Over and over again I will tell you that exercise will alleviate depression. I have not counted the number of times I repeat this slogan, but I hope it is ten, twelve, or more times. If repetition convinces you to exercise, I will use repetition.

It would be wonderful if I could make you experience, this minute, the positive mental changes you will attain after a six-week trial exercise period. Unfortunately, such miracles are beyond my power to perform. Only you can take the steps that lead to victory over depression. I urge you to take the time to read this book, believe what I tell you, and follow the path of physical activity that will help you defeat your depression.

John Stewart
Houston, Texas
April 1995

Depression—for those suffering from this mental disorder, the Webster definition is neither adequate nor accurate. Even medical practitioners often have difficulty characterizing the condition. Maybe it would be easier to visualize this condition. Along the side of the road or in a city alleyway, most of us have seen the beat-up, neglected, homeless, sickly, old mongrel dog. He limps on three legs, carrying the broken one. Mange scars cover most of his body except for a few patches of dirty yellow hair. His hip bones and ribs are fully visible, and one blind eye is glazed white from an old fight injury. Fleas make the wretched thing more miserable, except in the dead of winter. The cold of winter brings relief from flea bites and scratching, but then there is never a warm place to sleep. Depression feels like our old dog looks: hopeless.

For the purposes of this book we will call the mongrel Old Lucky—Old Lucky because if one constantly feels like this mongrel looks, I offer a possible and workable solution. That solution is physical activity. To satisfy our friends and contributors in the scientific community and the medical, including psychiatric, professions, I want to say at the outset that this is only one solution. By itself it will not be appropriate for everyone suffering from unipolar depression, which is downward depression. The other type of depression is bipolar depression, which is characterized by alternating up and down periods. Bipolar depression is also called manic-depressive illness. The severity of the depression has much to do with who can and who cannot benefit mentally from physical activity, and the severity of the depression may determine who has the present ability, physically and mentally, to begin any physical activity program. Other professional, psychiatric, and medical treatment, including medication, may be required in these more severe cases. But when the medical provider concurs, the patient should also follow this guide to physical activity as a reliever of depression.

Let us now imagine that a child befriended Old Lucky, fed him daily, and gave him a warm place to sleep. The parents of the child finally concluded that if the nasty, ugly old thing was going to hang around, they had best cure his mange and get rid of the fleas. Old Lucky is still an ugly mongrel, but now he is blessed with a home, three good legs, one good eye, and no fleas or mange. His new family has provided only a partial solution to his woes, just as physical activity may provide only a partial solution to depression.

Physical activity, or exercise therapy, for unipolar depression is possibly the only treatment that is fully in the hands of the person suffering from this mental disorder. It is not expensive, it is self-administered, and, above all, it works.

I use the words physical activity rather than the word exercise. Exercise brings to mind rows of young, physically fit people, clad in white shorts and sweat shirts, doing sit-ups, push-ups, and deep knee bends and running in place. We want to make you feel better than Old Lucky looks, not bore you into deeper depression. Calisthenics will work, but, believe me, there is a more interesting and enjoyable method.

Any physical activity program you decide to follow should be discussed and cleared with your medical practitioner. My purpose is to convince you that physical activity is one of the best, least expensive, and most rewarding methods for combating mild to moderate unipolar depression. If you are under the care of a psychiatrist or other medical doctor, psychologist, or other professional person, please share this book and its suggestions with that person.

Only a few years ago I was under the care of a psychiatrist for fairly serious depression. In addition to my weekly sessions with the psychiatrist, both a tranquilizer and antidepressant drugs were prescribed. At one of the weekly treatment sessions, my psychiatrist mentioned, almost in passing, that he would like to get me into an exercise program. Nothing else was said, and it was some months later that I accidentally found what physical activity could and can do for my condition. That day was a Saturday, and I was completing busywork at my office. A park and jogging trail are visible from my office window, and I decided to walk outside before driving home. I walked, maybe strolled is a better word, a three-mile loop from my office and back. I thought little about it, but the next time work was at a standstill I repeated the stroll. Weeks later and again on a Saturday, I walked the loop twice. That's six miles! Admittedly, I rested twice, but I was privately proud of walking six miles. At the rest stops I sat on a park bench, had a cigarette or two, and enjoyed being outdoors. This strolling habit continued on an irregular basis for about three months.

Because my path was next to a jogging trail, I was often passed by young, muscular, exercising joggers, male and female, who all resembled Greek gods. These young Greek gods were running the same distance (three miles) that I was strolling, and I usually required at least two rest stops to complete the three-mile loop. Soon I began to wonder how far I could run. I knew that because I smoked, drank, and weighed forty-five pounds too much, it certainly would not be the entire three-mile loop. I thought to myself, "Maybe half the loop." The perfect time to run was slow in coming because I wanted the trail to be deserted of the Greek gods. During this waiting period, I quickened the pace of my stroll to that of a legitimate walk, and I stopped only for one cigarette on the entire three-mile route.

The deserted day finally came! I set out to run at least half the loop, but I lasted less than one-eighth of a mile. That's bad! Very bad! In spite of this disappointment, I noticed that the walking made me feel better. In what way I felt better was difficult to describe then, as it is now—just better mentally. Maybe it is like Old Lucky: spending a few days without fleas, I definitely felt better mentally.

After finding I could not run with the Greek gods, I decided to air up the tires on my old bicycle and try riding it. The first weekend ride was with my daughter. On this maiden ride I had to stop and lie down to rest twice before completing fifteen miles. I couldn't run and I couldn't cycle. All I could do was walk. But then I began to blend the walking with a little running, and when possible I biked alone on the weekends. When you bike alone, no one has to wait for you.

It was finally obvious, even to me, that the limited physical activity was helping me mentally, and reasoning that more would help me feel even better, I wanted to do more. I wondered, "If I felt a little better mentally from this minute amount of activity, what must the Greek gods feel like mentally?" I reasoned they would feel like Old Lucky with no fleas in the summer and a warm place to sleep in the winter. At this point the unthinkable happened. I joined a gym!

Keep in mind that, so far, my physical activity consisted of walking two or three times a week, sometimes jogging a few steps of each mile walked, and taking a short bike ride once or twice a month. Even this limited physical activity was working against what my doctors had diagnosed as moderate to severe depression. No one told me it was helping, or why it was helping. I just felt it.

The therapeutic benefits of physical activity on unipolar depression had never been explained to me, but my own experience was making me curious. I had heard the phrase "runner's high," but I could not run more than three dozen steps, so that could not be the feeling affecting me. Was walking really helping me mentally? Would more be better? Should I try something else?

Now that I had invested in a health-club membership and bought a pair of walking shoes, some walking shorts, and two colorful T-shirts, I opted to do more. I had no proof that my limited physical activity was helping me mentally. Curiosity and the desire to feel even better prompted my decision to do more.

Even now it is difficult to describe the mental change without using the analogy of Old Lucky. It's like no fleas, no mange, a full stomach, a caring owner, and a warm place to sleep. What could be better?

After another seven months of flying blind, I began to do some research on why this physical activity was changing my depressed state. My first step was to define in my own mind the two major forms of depression. I asked several medical doctors who work in the mental health field to explain the difference between unipolar and bipolar depression. I came away with the explanation that unipolar depression, which is the most common, is a mood disorder that causes low, gloomy, despairing, hopeless, and certainly helpless feelings. The despair can be constant and reach extreme lows, to the point of suicide in severe cases. Bipolar depression, or manic depression, is a less common mood disorder in which periods of depression are often followed by periods of manic behavior. During the manic stage the person's behavior is characterized by a persistent "high" or by irritability and agitated moods. Loss of self-control and judgment, with racing thoughts, rapidly changing thought patterns, impulsive behavior, and greatly inflated ideas about one's own capabilities are only a few of the symptoms. I found no research that concludes that physical activity is helpful to those suffering from bipolar depression. Other parts of this book will explain what the scientific community believes to be the reason for mental improvement induced by physical activity, and I will outline different programs and give you a beginning point and a pattern to follow to help overcome depression. It certainly is not my intention to build the body beautiful, help you lose weight, improve the contour of your physique, or even improve your physical condition. The purpose is to use physical activity as one of the proven tools to lessen, and perhaps defeat, mental depression.

Do all who suffer from depression realize they are affected by this mental disorder? Certainly not! Unfortunately, most cases go undiagnosed and untreated. The symptoms and feelings of depression are often confused with a perceived physical problem. Many people who suspect that they may be affected by depression find it difficult to discuss possible mental problems with their physician. There are also a variety of physical disorders that mimic some of the symptoms of depression—to name only a few: diabetes, hypoglycemia, influenzas, mononucleosis, hepatitis, multiple sclerosis, and chronic-fatigue syndrome.

If you suspect depression but have not been professionally diagnosed, do not diagnose yourself. Seek professional help. Physical activity is effective against depression, but the same exercise treatment can be life threatening if some physical disorders are present.

The American Psychiatric Association first published the *Diagnostic and Statistical Manual* in 1952. Its purpose was to standardize a set of definitions for psychiatric illnesses and specify which symptoms and how many of them had to be present in order to make a particular diagnosis. The updated version, *DSM III*, published in 1980, contained

494 pages and covered 187 disorders. The criteria for a major depressive episode and a manic episode are printed in the appendix. This material is worth reading, but it is not a tool for self-diagnosis. Diagnosis must be done by a qualified, trained professional.

In each chapter of this book, and often after a few paragraphs, I will encourage you to set the book aside and go walk, go jog, or do whatever your present physical ability will allow. Why not walk for thirty minutes now? If not right now, then sometime today. If you are a reader who never finishes this book but one who starts and continues a physical activity program, I have accomplished my goal and so have you. This may sound like presidential candidate Ross Perot in the 1992 election campaign, "Just go do it!" Now!

Unlike me at the outset of my program, you will have the benefit of knowing that physical activity is an effective treatment tool for improving the mental state and mood of those suffering from unipolar depression. You have my experience, which largely was gained without the knowledge later acquired from reading the scientific studies, and you have the assurance gained from the scientific work. This worked for me, and it will work for you.

Before discovering the scientific work published in professional journals, I found a small ad in the *Wall Street Journal* for a booklet published by the Will Rogers Institute and titled, *What Everyone Should Know About Depression*. I requested the booklet and found it basic and helpful, but one small sentence especially caught my eye. The sentence read, "Get some exercise to help work off bottled up tension, relax, and sleep better." I promptly called the Will Rogers Institute to ask whether the institute had done any research on the effect exercise has on depression. It had not, but the director was kind enough to ask medical doctors associated with the institute to uncover articles on the subject. Shortly thereafter a computer listing of some fifteen articles arrived by mail, and a quick trip to the medical library opened my eyes to the experimental scientific and medical work being done.

SUMMARY OF SCIENTIFIC STUDIES

It works! It works! It works!

Basically, every research report I read concluded that physical activity creates a positive mood change for those people suffering from unipolar depression. "It works! It works! It works!" is a phrase I used one day while talking to a young lady employee of our firm. She observed me copying articles from medical journals on depression and related topics and confided that she had been under treatment for some years. We discussed the fact that she was not able to function without antidepressant medication, which was no longer proving effective for her. After our conversation I copied and gave to her two articles on physical activity and the curative effects it often produces for those suffering from unipolar depression. I also suggested that she discuss the subject with her doctor to see if he believed some regular exercise might help. Weeks went by before I asked whether she had talked to her doctor or started an exercise program. Her reply was that the doctor was indeed in favor of exercise. She had read the articles I had given her, and she really believed that she would feel better if she did exercise. However, she had not yet started, and the antidepressant medication was still of little benefit. That was when I shouted, "It works! It works! It works!" No doubt I sounded like a tent preacher, but my outburst prompted some action. She finally made the effort, and at last report physical activity was working for her. Her physical activity program was alleviating her depression.

In their book *Overcoming Depression,* Demitri and Janice Papolos mention the late-night TV talk-show host Dick Cavett. Cavett is quoted as saying, "What's really diabolical about it [depression] is that if there were a pill over there, ten feet from me, that you could guarantee would lift me out of it, it would be too much trouble to go get it."

I feel strongly that physical activity is one such pill for curing unipolar depression, but, as in Dick Cavett's case, what prompts the depressed person to walk the ten feet and take the first pill? I hope the results contained in these studies and experiments will act as a catalyst to prompt your action.

Most scientific studies and experimental results are published in journals normally available only to the medical community. The abundance of physical activity research and its publication has, in my opinion, prompted more medical practitioners to prescribe exercise as one treatment for unipolar depression. However, it is unfortunate that this information remains inaccessible to the general public. Those suffering from depression might more readily accept physical activity as a self-directed and self-conducted treatment for depression if only they knew more about it. As far back as 1984 one researcher estimated that more than one thousand studies have examined the psychological effect of exercise. By now there are surely twice that number, but still few of the results reach the lay reader.

By summarizing a few studies here in understandable language, I hope to convince those suffering from depression that physical activity will alter their depressed mood for the better. These positive results seem to be true for those taking antidepressants and tranquilizers as well as those using no medications.

For the most part, the studies I have summarized used real people as subjects and divided them into at least two groups. One group, the experimental group, exercises. The other group, the control group, does not. The depression level of each individual in each group was measured before, during, and after the exercise program. Without exception, the depression level of those in the exercise group improved over that of those in the control group.

Other medical studies have concentrated on the increased production of certain hormones by the body during and after exercise. Many such studies have used athletes as the subjects. However, one study conducted in Boston used several nonathletic, rather stocky, normal women. Using exact and intricate blood analysis techniques, researchers found that exercise induced the body to produce a greater amount of beta-endorphin and beta-lipotropin, both of which are hormones believed to influence diverse functions linked to the body's energy balance including appetite, thermoregulation, and reproduction.

Beta-endorphin, a naturally occurring opiate, is thought to be the chemical that produces the so-called runner's high. During exercise, laboratory animals produce higher levels of dopamine, norepinephrine, and serotonin. These seem to be the pleasant, or good, brain chemicals, and they are the compounds that various antidepressant drugs are known to impact.

Curiously, both regular exercise and antidepressant drugs require three to five weeks to begin to alleviate depression. Some researchers suspect that exercise not only prompts the body to produce more of the good brain chemicals, but the same exercise may cause the body to burn off stress hormones such as cortisol. It is almost impossible to be "stressed out" after running two or three miles, so maybe we have workable proof of this burn-off hypothesis.

This complex human brew-master capability needs to be used. The brew-master function of our body may resemble functions of other organs and muscles of the body. If they are not used, they become weak and puny. Who would want a puny brew-master?

It is unfortunate that there is no absolute proof that exercise causes the body to produce more of chemical A or hormone B or that either A or B will cure depression. As the scientific community continues to work, it will surely unlock these mysteries, although the answer will probably not be as simple as A and B.

Yet other theories suggest that the temporary increase in body temperature caused by physical activity may reduce certain receptor activity in the brain. The job of these receptors is to receive, lock onto, and then relay messages transmitted from cell to cell in the brain. If some receptors are less active at doing their assigned tasks, this phenomenon may cause the relief noted after exercise. This so-called down-regulation effect, in which the binding sites become less abundant, has been reported after treatment with most antidepressant drugs as well as with electroconvulsive therapy (ECT), also called electroshock.

The detection and evaluation of chemicals and hormones in the blood streams of exercising individuals prove that increased levels of many substances are attained. Which chemicals and hormones are produced and to what extent they cause mood changes are still unclear. But such testing does indicate that an actual chemical change takes place to help alleviate the depressed mood and, in fact, that physical activity brings on the elevated production of these hormones.

The appendix contains a primer plus a summary of four experiments that prove to me that exercise is a wonder drug for combating the symptoms of unipolar depression. The first article in the appendix is not the result of an experiment but a primer for the general practitioner or family doctor who may need to treat depression and anxiety using exercise therapy.

If you are already convinced that exercise is a therapeutic wonder drug for depression—a believer, so to speak—continue with the next section and read the appendix when time permits. If you still have doubts that physical activity is a therapy that will alleviate your depression, please spend the little time needed to read the studies. I need to convince two types of people. The first type—the believers— upon entering an airplane, asks if it will fly. Upon receiving a "yes" nod from a flight crew member, believers take their seats, ready to go. The second type—the doubters—wonder if the plane will fly and request an in-depth explanation of how the plane will become and remain airborne. If you are a believer, get on with the nuts and bolts and find out what you should be doing. Today you should be sweating and breathing hard. If you are a doubter, requiring knowledge of the whys and wherefores of physical activity as a cure for the symptoms of depression, read the appendix—but plan to get hot and sweaty tomorrow.

As you progress with a physical activity program and begin to feel better mentally, you may become curious, as I did. Many questions arise. What's happening to me? Is this feeling normal? Am I doing this correctly? Should I seek other, supplemental treatment? Should I tell someone that this works? Should I continue exercising forever? What happens if I quit? Or, at some point, am I well now? As these questions arise, obtain a copy of *The Exercise Prescription for Anxiety and*

Depression. The author, Keith W. Johnsgord, PhD, is a practicing psychologist, a teacher, and a researcher who often uses exercise therapy to treat depression and anxiety disorders. He has done research in the area and is knowledgeable about the research work of others. His professional knowledge about exercise therapy is sharpened by his own experiences as a distance runner. His superb work, published by Plenum Press, is directed toward the medical practitioner, the researcher, and the individual suffering from depression or anxiety. Do not overlook this book—eventually you will need answers to your questions.

Now it is the time for those who ask whether it will fly and what makes it fly to board the plane. We're ready to take off!

LEARN FROM THE "OLD GOAT"

The facts presented in the scientific studies should convince anyone that physical activity will produce positive mood changes for those of us suffering from unipolar depression. Being convinced is one half of the equation; getting the job done on a continuous basis is the other important half. The "Old Goat," as I'm referred to by some of my young workout partners, can help you with the second half of the equation. This Old Goat has some practical knowledge, gained while doing, that can help you with the doing part of your equation.

WHAT OUR PSYCHIATRIST FRIENDS SAY

Those professionals who minister to depressed patients seem to agree that a physical activity program for those suffering from unipolar depression will do wonders for them mentally. Without taking a breath or even blinking an eye, these same professionals express the fact that encouraging depressed people to work out is one thing, but getting them to do it is quite another matter. No doubt depressed people, whether or not they are receiving professional treatment, are a most unlikely group to embrace the idea of physical activity. Encouraging depressed people to be physically active is like asking our canine friend Old Lucky not to scratch his fleas. This proposed activity sounds like a good idea, it may do some good, and it may even be an important self-help method of virtually eliminating depression. In addition, it might give one the energy and clarity of thought to work through other underlying problems. All this could possibly be true, but where is the proof? Surely everyone realizes that I don't have the energy or determination to do something that is good for me, especially right now. These underlying thoughts are universal on the part of depressed people. Why do it? Should I do it? Can I do it? Will I do it? I know these four thoughts.

From first-hand experience, let me assure you that physical activity works wonders in relieving depression. If my experiences are not sufficient to convince you, I have already shared results of scientific studies that help substantiate what I have said, done, and felt. Amazingly, physical activity begins to help mentally in a matter of days, not weeks, not months, but days.

To answer your four questions:

1. Why do it? In the simplest terms, depression interferes with the normal functions of life. Those things that used to bring pleasure no longer seem to. Why then would one not try this low-cost, self-help method of treatment? Why not?

2. Should I do it? If you are under professional care, the answer is simple. Ask your practitioner. If, like many depressed people, you are not currently under professional care, then check with your medical doctor for any physical impediments, ask the doctor's opinion, and give it a try.

3. Can I do it? I outline programs that start where you can start. If you can walk one city block, please start with me. Remember, the Old Goat is not trying to decrease your time in the mile run, reduce your weight, or change your body contour. The sole goal is to demonstrate to you, personally, that physical activity will help you mentally.

4. Will I do it? The answer to that question is up to you. In this book I will demonstrate that this method works, I will describe the pleasure and rewards that return to you mentally, and I will assure you that the time you spend in therapeutic physical activity will become more and more valuable and dear to you. Unlike the Marine Corps, I am not asking for a two-year commitment, and I am certainly not looking for only "a few good men." I'm addressing those who seek a

self-directed solution to debilitating depression. Why not try this method for just three weeks and see how you feel. You can accomplish this short trial period if you approach it one day at a time.

If you skipped forward to the appendix and read the summary of several experiments, you no doubt noticed that the majority of depressed people are physically unfit; the figure may be as high as seventy percent. The other group, the remaining thirty percent, may appear fit or even be fit, often resembling the Greek gods that pass me daily on the jogging trail. Physically unfit does not always mean the excess body fat that one carries around. Some people who possess wonderfully active metabolisms can burn food at a rapid rate with limited physical activity, and little of what appears to be excess calorie intake is stored as fat. The phrase he or she is "skinny as a rail" was probably invented to describe these metabolically active individuals. Physical appearances can be deceiving when it comes to evaluating physical and mental fitness. There are thin depressed people who are physically unfit. There are thin depressed people who are physically fit. There are heavy depressed people who are physically unfit, and there are heavy depressed people who are physically fit. There are teenagers and even pre-teenagers, fit and unfit, who suffer from depression. The slithering course of depression seems not to be concerned about the physique of the body it invades. It is entirely possible that, after the onset of depression and the mental consequences it brings, many people become unfit because the spirit to be active is lacking.

Those mental health practitioners who prescribe and actually engage in physical activity with their patients have a great advantage when prescribing the correct activities. They can judge and test the patient's fitness level. They can decide whether the exercise should be a group sport or a solitary activity. They can dictate the number of days for aerobic activity and the number of days dedicated to strength training. If medication is being used by the patient, they will know the side effects and the possible consequences of strenuous physical activity combined with the particular medication. Above all, the mental health practitioner can continue to search for and help correct the possible underlying cause of the patient's depression.

Unfortunately, when one writes about the positive mental effects produced by physical activity, no single person can be addressed. The writing has to address the majority. The majority of depressed people are physically unfit and that group is addressed often in this book. If you fall in the minority, suffer from depression but are physically fit and active, other useful information can be found in the following pages.

This point was illustrated through the action of a friend who gave an early draft of this book to a colleague. He described her as about thirty-five, mother of two boys, a working partner in a family-owned business, extremely attractive and trim, a runner, and a good conversationalist who was often the center of attention at social functions. "Why," I asked, "would she want to read this book, especially in draft form?" He continued that this seemingly perfect young woman had suffered from depression beginning in high school but had brought it under control with physical activity and psychotherapy. It seemed to me that this young, successful woman had everything under control and that her reading what I had written at that early stage would be like my preaching to the choir.

Within weeks both my friend and I received a thank-you letter from her. From the letter it was possible to tell she had given the book a thorough reading. As one who already uses physical activity for mental health, she had several constructive suggestions. Her last paragraph taught me why a good preacher always turns and speaks a few words directly to his choir. She said, "Since I started running, depression is a thing of the past and I truly believe it will remain so. My problem has always been justifying the time I spend running. Because of my family and business responsibilities, I have felt more than a little guilty about devoting the required time to myself exclusively. The thoughts expressed in your writing made me realize that I cannot shoulder my enjoyable and rewarding, but often demanding, family and business responsibilities unless I do run."

If you are in the minority, the choir, please continue to read. If you uncover just one good applicable thought, this short book will be worth your time.

WHERE YOU START

If you do in fact fall in the category of physically unfit, the starting point is walking. As a minimum, walk for thirty minutes each day this week. Walk briskly, but do not speed walk. Do not use leg weights, and do not carry hand weights. Simply walk like a human being for half an hour. Thirty minutes is the minimum, but if time can be found, walk twice daily—thirty minutes each time. Any time of day is fine—before work or before other daily activity begins, at lunch, or in the evening. Remember that this is your time, so do your best to enjoy it. Select different routes for different days, if possible. Look around and smell the flowers, but keep walking. Many experts believe swimming is the perfect exercise, and it may well be, but walking comes close, so take this program seriously. It does good: it moves your heart rate up above normal, it uses leg and back muscles, it burns calories, and it may prompt your body to produce those chemicals or hormones that cause positive mood changes. Above all, it will make you feel better.

Often, depressed people feel like Old Lucky on a cold winter night. About all they feel capable of is to lie down, curl up in a ball, and hope to fall asleep. This is exactly the time when walking your thirty minutes does the most good, and it is the time when walking may be the most difficult. I know how difficult it might sound to take a thirty-minute walk when you feel this way. It is in fact difficult, but the difficulty is mental, not physical. This is the time when you have to believe that physical activity will help. If you will make the effort a few times, you will soon have the proof. You can actually walk your way out of this cold-winter-night mood.

Walking takes no new ability; we all know how to walk. If you are physically unfit, I suggest that you walk for a full six weeks before trying any jogging or running. In this time, your leg and back muscles will toughen up, and you will gain body and leg strength.

Again, as a minimum, I ask that you begin at the thirty-minute level. No particular distance is required, but if time permits during the day, I ask that you walk two times daily for thirty minutes each time. If that cold-winter night mood approaches, you should abandon what you are doing and walk for thirty minutes. This six-week, seven-days-a-week, walking program is designed to combat your depression. It is the beginning place for those who are currently physically unfit, and it will help lead you into more strenuous activity.

It is important that you walk at a pace that elevates your heart rate above the resting rate. A later section will tell you how to measure your heart rate.

For the first six weeks my one hope is to convince you that this thirty minutes to one hour a day of physical activity will have a positive effect on your mental-well being. Believe me, it will. Do not, however, expect noticeable side effects, such as weight loss or greater stamina, in this early period.

After this six-week period of walking, you will combine some short runs with the walking. If you feel physically fit and in condition to run short distances, you might want to read the Walk/Jog section and start there.

MULTIPRONG APPROACH

Most scientific studies that deal with the effect physical activity has on depression use a form of aerobic activity, such as walking, running, stationary cycling, and swimming. This aerobic activity produces an easily measurable component for the tests. That is, the increased cardiovascular gains can be easily measured, as can the decrease in depression scores, for those involved in the tests. Thus two components can be measured: depression scores, measured by various psychological tests, and physical condition, measured by tests that determine the maximum capacity of one's lungs. Both groups of tests can be administered before, during, and after completion of the physical activity program. Follow-up studies can be conducted months after the completion of any program. Because of this historic tendency toward aerobic exercise, some believed that aerobic activity was the only form of exercise that produced a positive effect on depression scores. Within the last five years more tests have been conducted using weightlifting as the exercise medium, and, for the most part, the results have shown that both aerobic exercise and weightlifting have the same positive effects on those suffering from depression.

My recommended physical activity program encompasses both aerobic activity and anaerobic activity, such as weightlifting (strength training). This combination creates a more flexible and enjoyable overall program. Use the suggestions contained in this book to develop the program that will be the most helpful to you and that will fit your schedule, ability, and liking. Ideally, I hope you will adopt an aerobic activity for four days of the week and a weightlifting regimen for three days. For this purpose, weightlifting is progressive resistance training (use of exercise machines). These machines are accessible in most health clubs, gyms, physical fitness establishments, schools, and the YMCA. If, however, these exercise machines are not available, use the section on strength training at home to achieve similar goals.

All exercise programs start at a slow and reasonable pace for several reasons. First, the slow and steady method avoids injury; second, if you have a persistent pain, you can check with your physician before an injury develops; and finally, if you are currently under professional care for depression, you can ask your practitioner for an opinion and comments about the program you have elected to follow. Let me repeat that you should check with your medical practitioner before starting any exercise program. The doctor may find it necessary to run tests to determine your current physical condition and possibly to make adjustments to the program you are considering. This discussion with your physician is important if you suspect or know of any possible physical impediment to an exercise program. Before this program is over, you will be sweating, breathing hard, stretching, pulling, lifting, pushing, squatting, panting, and probably cursing at times, but you will eventually love it all. The plan is to use physical activity to help you mentally, but by all means check with your physician about your ability to do these things.

The last reason for starting slowly is practical and relates to what has been learned about depressed people. There are exceptions, but the majority of people suffering from depression are sedentary. They no doubt feel like Old Lucky looks, but they physically resemble a good old house dog—a wonderful pet, but overweight, built like a shoebox with a head and four protruding legs, yet without enough energy to even growl at the postman. Exceptions do occur. Some depressed individuals are physically active, lean, and mean and in fact resemble the Greek gods that always passed me on the jogging trail. Perhaps these fit people can glean other useful information from this book.

In addition to your daily thirty-minute walk, you have another important project: to find and join a gym or health club that has weight machines. Since the advent and blossoming of the physical health industry, one can find a club, gym, or spa on virtually every corner. By contrast, just twenty-five years ago in my town, there were only two weight rooms. One was the main branch of the YMCA, and the other was Ron's Boxing Club & Weight Parlor. This establishment was down an alleyway in a less than desirable part of town, and Ron checked everyone at the front door. Ron was also the only instructor in the place, and everyone had to contend with his cigar smoke to take advantage of the instruction. His bookmaking activity caused the demise of the club even before the keen competition that now exists arrived in town. We've come a long way in the availability of health clubs and gyms, so try to make a wise choice when you join one.

After you have searched out a club located conveniently for you, obtain at least the following information:

• What is the cost, either monthly or yearly? Is there a membership contract involved? Is there a trial membership?

• Does the club have a beginner's class that teaches the proper use of the weight machines, or are instructors available to teach new members individually?

• Does the club have programs designed for beginners that teach the use of the equipment, then recommend a training course, and finally chart the progress?

• What other physical activity courses and classes are offered by the establishment?

• What are the weekday and weekend hours of the club?

Thoroughly research the club, and if possible use a trial membership program to ascertain if the chosen facility will fit your need.

WHAT TO WEAR

Most—not all, but most—depressed people lead an inactive lifestyle. Without physical activity, snacks and drink soon produce overweight, depressed people. Again, not all people suffering from depression are physically unfit and overweight, but enough fit that description that I wanted to include this section on clothing.

In warm weather, exercise clothing should be as skimpy as permitted by local law-enforcement agencies: such clothing allows perspiration to evaporate rapidly, and evaporation in turn cools the body. If, however, you resemble the Pillsbury Dough Boy, as I did, or you fit the description used by Garrison Keillor when he described a prominent citizen of Lake Woebegone, "His stomach was so large that it deserved a separate introduction," you, like me, are probably not inclined to appear in public wearing skimpy skintight garments. I surely faced this dilemma.

During cool months it is possible to cover up the large, lily-white body with a sweat suit or warm-up suit, but the warm months present a more difficult problem. There are lightweight sweat suits made of cotton knit similar to that used in T-shirts, and these garments are excellent for summer walking and running. Originally, I wore a pair of lightweight cotton pants with an elastic waistband and an extra-large T-shirt that was ample to cover most of the Dough Boy. The other people on the jogging trail where I walked were in running shorts and tank tops, but that attire was simply out of the question for me.

I have known men and women who wanted to exercise but who were too self-conscious to start because of their physical condition. You cannot let that happen because physical activity is much too important. As a by-product of your physical activity, your physique will eventually change, but do not let a self-conscious attitude about your present build stand in your way now. Today go through your closet to see what you might feel comfortable wearing. If you can't find anything suitable, visit a sporting-goods store and shop until you find the correct attire.

Since the disappearance of my unneeded forty-five pounds, my attitude toward other heavy people on the jogging trail has changed. Now when I see them I wish them well and hope I see them day after day because I know the effort it takes to be there.

Find the garments that will make you feel comfortable, do not be overly self-conscious, and get out there.

Currently, both walking shoes and running shoes are readily available. Either will work if they fit properly and do not rub blisters. If you shop for new shoes, opt for running shoes because our program will encompass both walking and jogging. A good fit is the important ingredient.

SLOW, CONSISTENT APPROACH TO PHYSICAL TRAINING

When one discusses strength or endurance training with coaches and professional trainers, a loosely defined formula relating to personal progression seems to emerge. The formula suggests that increases in weights, distances, or times should come at regular intervals and be of a predetermined amount. One might hear several formulas around the gym or on the jogging trail: If you do bench presses with sixty pounds and have progressed to twelve repetitions, you should increase the weight to seventy pounds, even if only eight reps can be accomplished at the new weight. If you jog for two miles at a ten-minute pace for about thirty running days, try to decrease your time to nine and one-half minutes or increase the distance by one-half mile. If you walk two miles a day at a fifteen-minute pace, try to add the third mile at the end of the second month while retaining the fifteen-minute pace. This slow and cautious progression has proved a good tool for virtually all physical training, and this programmed progression is often used when training for a particular athletic event. You, however, are using exercise as a therapeutic tool, so do not dwell excessively on this type of programmed progression. I have found that consistency is vastly more important than improvement in weight, time, or distance. Maintaining only consistency and setting no predetermined goals for improvement, in time you will note a physical improvement. But the mental improvement and positive mood change will start almost immediately.

Slower progress also guards against injury. Sometimes a pulled or strained muscle can interrupt what was to become a daily physical activity program. Equally important for avoiding injury is stretching before and after physical activity. You will no doubt learn some stretches by observing those participating in the same activity as you. Use the stretches you observe. A complete book on stretching, titled, of all things, *Stretching*, written by Bob and Jean Anderson and published by Shelter Publications, Inc., of Bolinas, California, provides good stretching exercises. You should order a copy and review the chapters concerned with your activity. Proper stretching before exercise not only loosens your muscles and lengthens the muscle fibers, it also just plain feels good.

Because consistency is the most important factor in your physical activity program, it is important to avoid any injury. Some muscles, after initial exercise, will be sore and tender, but this soreness should subside within forty-eight hours. If, however, pains occur in your joints, hips, or back, stop your exercise or slow to a pace where the pain subsides. Joint injuries can take forever to heal.

Consistency in therapeutic exercise means engaging in some form of physical activity every day of the week. Personal experience convinces me that a light workout such as a one-mile walk is much better mentally than no activity. Trainers and coaches usually recommend that a hard workout be followed by a day of rest. This gives the exhausted muscles time to recuperate. In the case of therapeutic exercise, I believe a hard workout should be followed by light activity the next day. For instance, if you work hard on the weight machines on Monday, make it a point on Tuesday to walk one or two miles. And remember to enjoy walking.

To accomplish a consistent physical activity program, it is important to have several exercise programs in your repertoire. To begin, try only one activity: walking, running, lifting weights, or swimming, for example. Add to this beginning activity as soon as possible because various activities add to the overall enjoyment of the program and help sustain a seven-days-a-week program. If, as the scientific community suspects, physical activity prompts the body to manufacture chemicals and hormones that produce a positive mood change, then, in my opinion, one should use that internal manufacturing capability every day. This human capability is not like a baseball pitcher's arm: it cannot be overused.

When you embark on a physical activity program and continue with it, an explanation might be required for family members or others close to you. My explanation has usually been that it simply "makes me feel better." Because a seven-days-a-week program requires a good deal of time, your family may need a more complete explanation. If need be, you can ask the inquiring person to read the section titled *To the Support Group*.

Summary advice from the Old Goat:

• Start slowly—don't push.

• Be consistent and vary your routine.

• Do something every day.

REWARDS

The feelings of depression are often suffocating. You truly feel like Old Lucky looks. The things that normally bring pleasure no longer do. Mentally, the dead of winter seems perpetual. I know this feeling, know it well, and know that it is real. Considering this mental state, participating in any physical activity may seem out of the question, and it may even be repulsive. I also know that feeling. Let me assure you that the rewards to you are there, this will work, and it does not take months. In only days you will begin to notice the difference. It is entirely possible to begin to feel a little better mentally on the first, second, or third day. The overwhelming reward to you is that you will feel better mentally.

Add to your program some artificial rewards that will add a little fun and sense of accomplishment. Use these self-rewards to help you stay on the track and become consistent with your chosen physical activity program.

After I discovered that simply walking was helping me mentally, I decided to keep track of the number of times per week that I walked for at least thirty minutes. My record-keeping ability was not great at that time, so I bought seven buttons. These were my markers. I carried all seven buttons in my pocket at the beginning of the week, and each evening, when I completed walking, I placed one in a small jar on the bathroom cabinet. It sounds trivial, but that jar filled with seven buttons began to represent time I was spending for myself. If by Sunday evening the jar contained seven buttons, I felt better than if only one or two were there. Seven buttons placed in my pocket Monday morning had the added effect of a constant reminder. I needed to walk. I needed to spend time to feel better. The buttons became my self-awarded medals for accomplishing the task. This simple method of measurement created no additional pressure to conform to a preset schedule, and it did not create guilt if the task was not completed. It did give me a measure of the time devoted to working against my foe—depression.

I did not keep track of weight loss or increased endurance. These were not, at that point, important goals.

Later, when I began working with the exercise machines, I bought buttons of different colors. I had white for walking and red for weightlifting. My goal then was four whites and three reds per week. Again, this method is simply a low-stress way of allotting time for yourself. If Old Lucky is combating fleas by scratching, you are combating mental fleas with physical activity. Use any small daily, weekly, or monthly reward that helps you.

When I was finally able to run more than a few steps at a time, I began to use a calendar to keep track of the miles run per week.

Believe me, the miles per week were small at first. Keeping a calendar was not as much fun as the buttons, so I decided that if after a month I was satisfied with the mileage results, I would buy something as a reward. Soon the closet was filled with colored T-shirts, my choice for the added reward. Eventually, I maintained a daily calendar in which I recorded all physical activity. Also noted were the days of no physical activity and the reasons, if any. An entry might read "No workout—business trip." I soon devised a code by the use of the symbols M+ and M–. These symbols related to my mental feeling and attitude after workouts. M+ was always the symbol used and noted in the calendar no matter what form of physical activity I did. It could be using weight machines, cycling, walking, running, or swimming. The very few M– were on days of no physical activity. By this time, however, the no-exercise days were few in number. I began to guard this exercise time from intrusion. It was my time. It was working and working big. I was doing it; I was in charge. No feelings of helplessness, no medication. I felt good, and I was confronting other problems as they came along. If only I could stay on the program that had evolved.

HOW TO STICK WITH IT

Physical activity programs, diets, and New Year's resolutions all attract many beginners and almost as many dropouts. It is estimated that of all those who start any physical activity program only fifty percent are still participating after one year. You, however, should have greater motivation than most beginners because this exercise program is for your mental well-being.

There are some methods that may help you to maintain an exercise program on a long-term basis. Read on to find the method that may work for you.

If you can afford the cost of engaging a professional trainer, do so. These professionals can be found by inquiring at health clubs, gyms, and YMCAs or by asking physical therapists or possibly your family doctor. You will probably want to interview several trainers. Look for a personality fit and decide how you feel about each candidate's qualifications and ideas for helping you. Explain in detail to your trainer why you are embarking on a physical activity program. You should ask that the trainer review this book. Your trainer may then decide to alter your program to better fit your needs. Your primary purpose is mental health, not to build muscle mass, increase endurance, lose or gain weight. These by-products of exercise will eventually evolve, but they shouldn't be goals when you start.

You and your trainer will probably settle on a two- or three-days-a-week schedule. This does not preclude you from walking, running, or other aerobic activity on the off days. The trainer should work with you on the proper method for both weight training and aerobic training. He or she will meet you at the gym or health club two or three hours a week for your individual workout. This instruction, individually designed for your needs, will make the workout safer, more enjoyable, and more productive. The trainer can judge the speed at which you should progress to help you avoid injury. It is important to learn the proper, safe, and most productive methods for all exercise, but especially for weight training. Another strong motivation is prepayment for training sessions. This "pocketbook" incentive will encourage most people to be there on time even when other things seem more pressing.

Take classes. If you look hard enough, you can find a class for everything. There are aerobic classes, bench aerobic classes, water aerobic classes, walking classes, swim classes, and martial arts classes, just to name a few. These classes and others are available through churches, health clubs, and YMCAs, and are often even sponsored by corporations. You can find the right class for your need if you only look. Classes of any kind create an incentive to show up and participate. Meeting new people is an additional reward of any class activity. Again, if your class meets once, twice, or three times a week, you should participate in a complementary activity on the other days. Every day do something—every day.

Bench aerobics is one of the best forms of body exercise. Some men have the misconception that bench aerobics is a female activity. It is not. More and more men are discovering this aerobic activity, and I have noticed more men enrolling in bench aerobic classes. Usually it takes several months before the men catch up with the women, if they ever do.

My first encounter with a class for sports training or exercise training was at the new gym. The bulletin board advertised a runners' clinic that would meet two times a week in the early morning at the roof track. The advertisement listed the subjects to be covered, which were stride technique, training methods, diet, cold-weather running, heart-rate monitoring, and conditioning for distance. I paid the thirty dollars, filled out the entry form, and waited until the first Wednesday of the following month, the beginning date.

I thought I was going to a lecture class that would cover most of the subjects, although the material did say meet at the track each Wednesday and Friday morning at 6:00 A.M.

At 5:50 A.M. on the first Wednesday of October I arrived at the gym, dressed warmly, and climbed the four flights of stairs to the roof track. When I opened the door to the track, which normally would be dimly lit and almost deserted, I found thirty or more runners warming up and stretching, clad only in shorts and T-shirts. The track was brightly illuminated with television lighting and a video camera, and an operator was stationed at either end of the oval track.

I quickly shut the door, turned on my heel, and thought, "Heavens, what have I gotten into now?" While I descended the stairs back to the dressing-room area, I remembered that I had not brought my extra-large T-shirt and the long cotton pants that were my walking and running attire. If I chose to go back up to the track and participate, I would have to dress in the skimpy white running shorts and the tight little T-shirts provided by the gym. I knew from experience that I would look exactly like Baby Huey, white diaper and all, dressed in the outfit provided. My choice was to leave for work two hours early or change into running clothes and make a fool of myself. I changed, then stopped by a mirror, where my suspicion that I looked like Baby Huey was confirmed, and finally climbed the stairs to the roof.

All the skinny little runners gathered in two groups for instructions from the coaches. I found a place at the rear of one group. I tugged and pulled at the bottom of my small T-shirt in hopes that the material would lengthen enough to cover most of my stomach before the running started and the video cameras made a permanent record of the event. The fabric gave a bit, but not nearly enough.

The instructions were to pin a number on the front and back of my T-shirt so that the video record could be critiqued later, then jog for fifteen minutes as a warm-up. Three runners at a time were to circumnavigate the track five times for the cameras. My earlier thought returned: "Old Goat, what have you gotten into now?" Five times around this track was half a mile; half a mile was near my limit for running. How could I stay equidistant from the runners in front of and behind me? I couldn't jog for fifteen minutes as a warm-up. To date my best running performance had been to jog for five minutes, walk for two minutes, then jog again. This was not going to be pretty: My exposed lily-white skin was turning pink from the early morning cold—maybe the video was in black and white.

The number pinned on my shirt front and back was 3, which meant that I was to go in the first group of runners. My thought returned: "Why didn't you leave and go to work early when you had the chance?" There was no escape, so Baby Huey, along with everyone else, started the fifteen-minute jogging warm-up. I walked twice during the warm-up, and most of the greyhounds lapped me several times. After the warm-up, the instructor hollered, "Number 1, go! Number 2 go! Number 3, go!" I ran all five filming laps, and the ordeal was over—over, that is, until the group video-viewing session scheduled for Friday morning. At the critique, when I first appeared on the TV screen, but before the coach could comment, I said "Here comes Baby Huey." The others in the room did more than chuckle, and the ordeal was finally over.

The next eight sessions were packed with valuable and useful information. The coaches were knowledgeable, and all the lean, thin greyhounds were helpful. I had a lot to learn, and this class turned out to be the correct way to learn.

Don't be shy or bashful about participating in something new. Most exercise or sports training classes are designed for the beginner. Even if one stumbles into an advanced runners' clinic as I had done, the new knowledge and friendships are worth the few moments of anxiety.

Get workout partners. If you have a friend or friends who participate in the physical activities you choose, the workout buddy system is helpful to all. The buddy system creates an added incentive to show up at the appointed time. It helps if your workout partners have the same ability or speed as you, but it is not absolutely necessary. My running buddy habitually leaves me in the dust. We do, however, meet at a particular time and place, we run the same course, and we meet in the parking lot after the run. Do not try to keep up with a workout partner if his/her ability is above yours. Work out at a pace you can maintain.

Participate in organized runs, walks, and cycling events. These organized events are fun and worthy of your participation. Most events are not designed exclusively for the superathlete or the Greek gods. Many organized events are designed to raise money for local charities or other good works; therefore, the sponsors expect and hope to attract the more numerous beginners. Many runs also have walks along the same course as the run or a shorter run for beginners. Most cycling events have several courses; often twenty-five-, fifty-, sixty-eight-, and one-hundred-mile courses are available to the rider. Some rides even have a ten-mile course for children and parents.

Buy in to the "T-shirt syndrome." At my first five-mile run, I made only two and one-half miles before it became necessary to walk. Between two and one-half miles and the finish, I had to walk twice. But I finally crossed the finish line as the race closed. Behind me were even a few people who I believed were in the race. I crossed the finish line, and I got to wear the T-shirt contained in the entry pack.

Much later, when I entered my first one-hundred-mile bike ride, I expected to finish because I had ridden sixty-eight miles the weekend before. At seventy-eight and one-quarter miles I died. I could not walk or ride the half-mile to the next rest stop. Two young riders who had already completed the one hundred miles and were then assisting in the pickup of the dead and wounded passed by me in their pickup truck. They recognized me as badly wounded and returned. One of the young men put my bike in the back bed of the truck and asked me to hop in the cab while he held the door open. Hop, I couldn't. The driver then pulled my arm and the doorman pushed from my rear. The air-conditioned cab felt great, and I thanked them for the comfort and the ride, but I also expressed my disappointment that I had been unable to finish the ride. The young driver said, "Hey, Dad, you made it seventy-five miles. How old are you anyway?" I corrected his mileage to seventy-eight and one-fourth and told him I was fifty-five years old, although I felt sure he was not a direct descendant. Then the young man who did the pushing from my rear replied, "Say, Dude, my dad is forty-three and I bet he can't do twenty-five miles—you did damn good for someone old." As we approached the finish line by air-conditioned pickup truck, I mentioned that I wanted to wear one of the ride T-shirts, but it just didn't seem right because I had to drop out at seventy-eight miles. The young driver spoke up, "Dad, you did seventy-eight and one-quarter miles—some of the dudes walking around here did only twenty-five or fifty." That lecture from my two young rescuers started the T-shirt syndrome. If I go, make the start, and try, I wear the event T-shirt.

The side effect from entering these events is the conditioning leading up to the event day. If you register for a three-mile run, I guarantee your mileage will increase during the thirty days before the run. Cycling will increase once you register for a bike event. In addition, it's fun and you meet new people.

Get a workout calendar. A workout calendar is an excellent tool to keep you in the groove, so to speak. A blank copy of a weekly calendar is produced at the end of this book. Make copies and use it as you see fit. Each of the days has a planning section and a doing section. Try to plan a week in advance and alter the plan depending on the weather and other circumstances. Each day when I pencil in the finished product, I try to grade the results from A+ to C. There are no Ds or Fs in my grading system. If you show up and complete the task, with even a minimum of effort, it is worth a C. If you really try, it is an A+.

You will notice an M+ in the lower right side of each day. This symbol represents a better mental feeling and attitude after completing your daily physical activity. If you do feel better, simply circle the M+. I hope you will be pleased and surprised with the number of circles in just the first two or three weeks.

MILIEU THERAPY

In the period between the First and Second World Wars, Winston Churchill reported repeated bouts with depression. He named his mood the "black dog"—as always, well-chosen words by "The Master." Part of his self-prescribed therapy was his hands-on construction of the now-famous brick wall at his country home and, of course, his painting. This type of milieu therapy can be important and helpful to you in your determination to stick with your exercise program. Milieu is defined as something that surrounds or affects an outcome but is not directly related to or does not directly affect the course. To you, this means volunteering—volunteering to assist at sporting events in which you cannot possibly participate, for example.

My first experience with this type of therapy was when I was asked to help do the setup work for a local triathlon. I reasoned that it would be interesting to watch the race afterward, but I soon found that I had volunteered for the unloading of an eighteen-wheeler the day before the race. Nonetheless, I traveled back out to the event site the next morning and saw many superb competing athletes. The second time I was asked to volunteer, I had grown a little wiser. Upon asking, I was told that I was to be the fourth backup photographer at the finish line during our local marathon. This task was not a task at all. I had a pass to the finish area and saw the start from a good location. All that was required of the four of us was to photograph the first five male and female finishers. Once that job was completed, I continued taking shots until the film was exhausted and later mailed the photos to each of the runners, reasoning that anyone who could run twenty-six miles deserved a picture of the finish. Physically, it was impossible for me to participate in these events, but just being there certainly had a positive mental effect.

CLUBS

There are almost as many clubs as there are classes. Clubs abound and cover virtually every physical activity. Certainly there are cycling clubs, but in most cities one will also find walking clubs, running clubs, and swimming, rowing, weightlifting, yoga, and skiing clubs, to name only the familiar ones. Investigate the clubs in your area that may focus on the physical activities you have chosen. Some will be listed in the telephone directory, but others will require some sleuthing on your part.

Our local biking club sponsors four country rides per month and has one weeknight sit-down meeting per month. Attending meetings and rides assures one of interesting and varied people as riding part-ners. Getting to know the interesting and unusual people is sometimes as rewarding as the activity itself.

This last spring was windy by any standard for our area, and biking in constant twenty- to twenty-five-mile-per-hour winds became very tiresome. I decided to try something new for a weekend activity until summer arrived, when only temperature, not winds, determines one's outdoor activity. I joined the local soaring club because flying sailplanes seemed interesting. The club brochure painted an even more interesting scenario. I first called the number listed and chatted with one of the instructors, who told me how the club functioned, the cost, location, and such. It was required that each member not only pay dues but also donate one day a month in labor. It seemed mowing runways and washing planes were reserved for new members. My contact further explained that the instructors and tow-plane pilots were club members and volunteers, which kept the cost to new mem-bers low. He told me about each piece of equipment owned by the club and mentioned, in passing, that one could fly gliders even if one had lost his/her power-plane rating because of a physical handicap. Finally he told me how to get to the airstrip, so the following weekend I drove there to meet one of the instructors at the appointed time.

During the drive I thought about the fact that soaring had little to do with physical activity, but the idea still had appeal. When I arrived, I found one automobile parked next to the country road and a sign that said, "Do Not Drive On The Runway." I couldn't make out the runway, but I parked and looked for some sign of life. Off in the distance was a shack. A few gliders were parked next to it. I walked through the wet grass toward this one possible sign of life. Once around the corner of the tin shack, I found three men sitting on the steps. Collectively they looked as if they had lost their best friend. I introduced myself by name and asked if any of them was an instructor. Only one man responded. He said, "The runway is too wet for the tow plane." After standing in silence for a few minutes, I decided that the wet runway was the reason for the trio's state of mourning. After a few more moments of silence I began to excuse myself for the walk back to the car. Then one of the mourners interrupted and said they were going to make a pot of coffee and I could stay if I liked.

The next four cups of coffee introduced me to three interesting people who turned out to be my instructors. Notice that I describe them as interesting, not physically fit. During our conversation over coffee, the telephone conversation of a few days ago took on real meaning, especially the instructor's statement that one can fly gliders after losing his power-plane license. Two of the gentlemen told me that they each had heart pacemakers; the other, however, had more visible defects. The patch over his left eye was obvious; less obvious was his artificial leg. Both were consequences of his first military plane crash—non-US military, I was informed, although that bit of information was unnecessary because I couldn't understand one out of ten words he spoke.

By the time the second pot of coffee was brewed, I felt at ease enough to ask the three if the club had any instructors with all body parts attached and functioning. No one took offense at my question, and they quickly informed me (hallelujah!) that the lady instructor, not then present, had all parts. But I was also told that she talked an awful lot. The brochure had described soaring as quite effortless, exhilarating, and relaxing. A talker didn't fit the bill, so I opted to schedule my first lesson with the foreign fellow, reasoning that although he had a few missing parts, there was no battery power required. The thought of being towed to an altitude of fifteen hundred feet and released from the tow plane and then depending on a small battery implanted in my instructor was not a relaxing thought.

Since the initial meeting the spring winds have died, so I am back to biking. But I now have nine landings to my credit, and I have been up with all four instructors, including the lady who talks too much. She does talk a lot, but with a beautiful French accent, so that works fine. Each of the four is an interesting, different person with thousands of flying hours and almost as many stories to tell.

Soaring is not physical exercise, but it can be justified because mowing the runway and washing the planes certainly are exercise. I need no justification, however, because the people are so much fun. I'm sure I'll be there until I need a pacemaker, and I'll enjoy every minute of it.

The Old Goat advises that once you start an activity—be it in a class, with a personal trainer, or as a club member—jump in the middle of it, be as active as possible, and don't participate from the borders or sidelines. Jump in and stay in!

SIDE EFFECTS

Important and good physical things begin to happen as the result of a prolonged physical activity program. Many of these changes are discussed by Dr. Charles Smith in his article titled, "Exercise—Practical Treatment for the Patient with Depression and Chronic Fatigue" (see the appendix). For now, let's overlook the physical changes and discuss a few personality changes I have noticed in myself and others.

Organization and use of one's time seems to improve as the physical activity program continues. I am not sure whether the improvements are the result of a better mental attitude or simply the need to block out one hour to one and one-half hours a day for a special purpose. Some planning is required even for your first thirty-minute walk, and the need to plan increases as the schedule intensifies. If you enter an organized walk/run or cycling event, even more personal planning and organization are required. First you have to sign up, then plan your training workouts, allot time for these, reserve rooms if it is an out-of-town event, attend any pre-race briefings, have ready the proper and necessary equipment, and finally be at the starting line on time. Even a three-mile fun walk requires most of the above-mentioned actions.

The word *titivate* is an old navy term. It means to spruce up, make tidy, or clean your assigned area. To make my physical activity sessions more enjoyable, I have found it useful to complete one last task at work. For you, it might be one or two small tasks that will make life a little easier when you return. Titivate your area before you leave for exercise. It helps.

Some psychiatrists believe depressed people have a tendency to neglect important tasks, duties, and obligations in their daily lives and often opt for an activity that is less demanding and more immediately rewarding than the important tasks facing them. This is somewhat like the young boy shooting baskets instead of doing his homework. This observation is probably correct in most instances. However, in the case of the physical activity program proposed here, the primary purpose is to correct mental depression. Alleviating depression is possibly as important as any life duty or obligation confronting most people.

If this book persuades you to devote time, effort, and energy to physical activity, I have accomplished my goal. Do not, however, neglect your other duties and obligations. My guess is that you will feel so much better mentally that both sets of priorities will get done in very good fashion. Mental well-being is not a side effect; it is your primary goal.

Humor is virtually lost by those suffering from depression. Once the physical activity has a little time in which to affect your mental attitude and mood, I feel sure some degree of humor will return. In my case even I found it humorous to be a 215-pound "Pillsbury Dough Boy" on the track with the Greek gods or in the weight room with the superhumans. Laughing at oneself might be part of the therapy.

The ability to stop and smell the roses also returns quickly. Early one morning while jogging, I noticed a 1937 yellow Packard convertible parked in the lot next to the park pavilion. I U-turned and approached the owner of the auto, who was dressed in attire of the 1937–38 era. He told me that a vintage auto show was to take place that day and went on to tell me more about his Packard and Packards in general. Because the owner of the beautiful yellow convertible was so friendly, I decided to hang around. That day I saw Cords, one Pierce Arrow, one Auburn, several more Packards, and several Studebakers. In the Ford line, there were T-Models, A-Models, and '37, '39, and '41 Fords. Great-looking Lincolns were shown, including Zephyrs and a fleet of little T-Birds. I spent that day viewing these magnificent machines and returned the next day. I blew two days of exercise and couldn't find my jogging partner, whom I lost at my U-turn into the parking lot, but I enjoyed two great days. Don't forget to stop and smell the roses, even if they smell like leather and finely crafted machinery. They may not be there the next time around.

"Scuttling about" is the term I use for the increased energy level one reaches after only a few weeks of physical activity. Webster's second definition of scuttle is "a quick shuffling pace." Scuttling is similar to scurrying, but a scuttler always has a mission in mind. Something needs to get done so that the big picture is complete or the final project is accomplished. Physical activity produces increased energy, which, in turn, can be used for more physical activity or for the accomplishment of other tasks.

Depression is often responsible for tolerance of the status quo. Depressed people may desire that things change but lack the energy to take the actions required to change their circumstances. Change requires action and action requires energy.

My daughter, the hyperactive, athletic career girl, is the number one "scuttler" I know. She attributes her high energy level to athletics, and this energy level is sometimes astounding to me. Her hobbies are triathlons, competitive swimming, and marathons. This in itself is amazing enough, because each event and the practice involved require great amounts of energy, but this group of hobbies also requires much "scuttling about" just to be there and participate. The logistics of travel, allotting time for practice, caring for her home, and earning a living all require energy.

During one ten-day period when I was asked to take care of her dog, I saw what this level of energy can accomplish. I also have witnessed the increased energy level of people when depression subsides and they are then able to initiate needed life changes. During this ten-day period, while I was dog-sitting, the girl jock worked late two nights to prepare for a trade show in Chicago. With another girl triathlete she planned to drive from Houston to Dallas for a triathlon on Sunday, but first they attended a college football game during the Saturday drive to Dallas. On Sunday both girls participated in the triathlon and were very satisfied with their times. After the event my daughter flew to Chicago for a five-day trade show. Manning a booth at a trade show is no easy task, but her plan was to run another triathlon on the following Sunday in Chicago. This schedule left Saturday free to rest and enjoy the sights. At 11:30 Sunday night I picked her up at the Houston airport and heard that she was pleased with her running times that Sunday morning. In contrast, I was tired and all I had done was dog-sit and report nightly by telephone that my animal charge was doing fine.

After talking with this female athlete and her athletic friends, I am persuaded that physical activity produces more energy. When you exercise, this phenomenon will happen to you, and you will use the added energy for many constructive endeavors.

It is said that regular physical activity helps us deal with stress. It does! It is said that regular physical activity helps us deal with anxiety. It does! Prove it to yourself by trying it, or you may have to listen to another of my stories.

There seems to be little need to write about the physical effects that will be part of your activity program because these subjects are covered and available in numerous volumes. Weight loss, muscle tone and heart capacity improvements, and even reversal of the aging process are all subjects of books that can be found in your local bookstore.

If the Old Goat obtained a few good side effects from exercise, think what might happen to you! You, too, will have the energy to "scuttle about."

BACKSLIDERS

In country Protestant churches in the rural South there is a classification of members known as backsliders. A backslider is a person who was once a good faithful member of the congregation, attended services regularly, met with the approval of the preacher and elders, gave sufficient money to the church, and could always be called on for most church functions. Backsliders are still members of the congregation, but they are showing signs of sliding downhill toward the ways of the devil. Perhaps they do not attend services as often as they used to, they may make excuses for not doing extra work for the church, and they may have even been seen at the local honky-tonk once, or once too often.

A good country preacher has a plan, and even a team of elders as assistants, that he can dispatch to make one or more rescue attempts on the backslider. The preacher is only doing his job, and, of course, it is more efficient to pull a backslider back toward the flock than it is to find a new member or possible convert.

Because physical activity is so important to the mental well-being of anyone suffering from depression, you, like the Southern preacher, need a predetermined plan in case you become a backslider. You will know the symptoms, but let me list several.

• You exercised only twice last week.

• You thought of errands that had to be done in your exercise time.

• You started an exercise workout but quit early several times recently.

• You had to go shopping during your normal exercise time.

• You went to have a drink at your normal exercise time.

• Several times recently you went home to nap during your exercise time.

Like the good country preacher, I know the backslider can be rescued by following a combination of predetermined methods. Some of the precautionary steps you might take are as follows:

• Have new, varied routines already worked out. If you are running, walking, or biking, have two new routes picked out and begin to use them.

• Have some "want to" projects and challenges ready to go. Do you want to learn to play tennis, swim, ice skate, or row?

• Find a new exercise partner or group.

• When you are thinking of avoiding an exercise session, try first to make it an abbreviated or light workout. A grade of C for an abbreviated workout is much better than a no-show.

• If some excuse causes you to miss your exercise one day, don't accept any excuse the next day. Never miss two days in a row.

• Always have something you are working toward—an organized run, a bike rally, a swim meet. Sign up for these events early—mark them in your calendar and number the days until the event day. When you know that there are only twenty days remaining until the starting time, each workout or practice secession becomes more valuable.

• Make a sticker, "Exercise Keeps Me Sane." Place it inside your calendar, inside your locker, or anyplace you will see it daily.

• If possible, vary the times of your physical activity. If your normal exercise time is late afternoon, schedule a couple of early morning workouts.

• Be a spectator at a sporting or athletic event. Try to find an event that you have never seen.

Like the good southern preacher, have your plans worked out ahead of time. It is likely that all of us will become backsliders at one time or another. There are no elders to make a rescue call on you, so know what your game plan will be.

SMOKING AND PHYSICAL ACTIVITY

A high percentage of depressed people still smoke in spite of the vast amount of research proving the ill effects of smoking. If you do smoke, do not assume that smoking precludes you from aerobic activity. It does not.

From a physical activity standpoint, smoking has at least two negative effects. It restricts the expansion of the arteries when your body needs oxygen-enriched blood, and the buildup of tars and chemicals in the lungs restricts their ability to absorb oxygen into the blood and carry away carbon dioxide when you exhale. If you are a competing athlete, smoking may preclude you from competing at the best level in your class; however, it does not preclude you from physical activity, even aerobic activity. Even if you consume several packs of cigarettes a day, you will slowly notice more endurance if your exercise program is structured properly and followed consistently for some weeks.

I am not here to change your personal habits except as they relate to physical activity needed to alleviate depression. Although I smoke I slowly moved from walking, to running a few steps at a time, then to running a mile and then eight miles. If I had decided that I must quit smoking before I ran that first step, I would probably still be in the throes of depression.

Other benefits may come in time, even cessation of smoking. Start the physical activity program.

ALCOHOL, DEPRESSION, AND PHYSICAL ACTIVITY

As they say in my part of the country, "You gotta listen, and listen hard." If one drinks to excess, he/she is confronting the "chicken or egg" problem. Is depression prompting excessive drinking, or is excessive drinking causing depression? We all know that alcohol is a depressant, and it is certainly not an ingredient that needs to be added to the chemical makeup or mood of anyone suffering from depression. When it comes to depression and alcohol, I feel there are only two types of drinkers: the As and the Ds. As are alcoholics; Ds are social drinkers of the lightest order. No Bs or Cs in my classification system. If you are an A, your drinking is interfering with other activities in your life. The Ds have a few drinks now and then, but these occasions can easily be skipped and they do not interfere with other life functions or duties. If, in this limited grading system, you fall into the As or suspect that you are coming close, other help will probably be required.

Alcoholism is most often treated through self-help programs and without medication in programs similar to those presented by Alcoholics Anonymous. AA begins each meeting with the verbal admission that you are an alcoholic. "My name is Jane Doe and I am an alcoholic." This frank admission in the company of others confronting and trying to defeat the same problem and addiction goes a long way toward the eventual cure.

It seems to be proved that practicing alcoholics, the As in my grading system, have a tendency to lie to themselves, their family, or other loved ones about their drinking and its effects. Here you cannot lie to yourself because you have to be the judge of how much help you need. You no doubt need help with depression, but do you need a different kind of help with drinking? If the answer is yes, AA keeps an open door. Make a telephone call, find the door, and walk through it.

The physical activity recommended in this book will help you with your alcoholism, but I doubt that it alone will be the cure to this addiction. Fighting the combination of depression and alcoholism is a formidable task, and you will need all the support and help obtainable. AA and some other private providers have treatment programs that work. Step one, of course, is the admission that you have an addiction and a problem with alcohol.

The two programs, physical activity for depression and treatment for alcoholism, can work hand in hand, but you will have to be the judge of your condition, and only you can be honest or dishonest with yourself.

PHYSICAL ACTIVITY AND THE PREVENTION OF DEPRESSION

I found little scientifically conducted research in the area of exercise as a preventive tool for depression, and when one thinks about it, that fact is understandable. Prevention, as it applies to medicine or mental health, means adopting and applying lifestyle changes, diet changes, vaccinations against known contagious diseases, and employment of protective medications. The changes recommended, or the medication and vaccinations prescribed, can be tested in animals, and sometimes in humans, exposed to a particular disease. The results can be tabulated and compared with those from another group also exposed to the same disease but not treated (a control group).

Unfortunately, depression has a winding, changing life of its own, making scientifically conducted prevention studies very difficult. Even the cause is not absolutely defined yet. Is it genetic, environmental, hormonal, learned, or a combination of some or all of these? Once the scientific community unravels the cause or causes, whether they be one, two, or ten in number, the prevention and cure should be fast in coming. In the meantime, we work with what we have and what we think, know, and suspect.

Physical activity could well be a prevention for unipolar depression. Many physically positive results of exercise have been measured, documented, and proved. Normal, nondepressed people report positive mood changes when exercising, as reported in "Swimmers Really Do Feel Better." There is a chance that exercise could decrease the likelihood of the onset of depression in those susceptible to depression, as exercise now is prescribed as a treatment for the prevention of heart disease in patients deemed susceptible to that disorder. Fortunately, attempts to determine who is susceptible to heart disease have led to the formation of a series of questions and medical examinations. Are you overweight? Is there a history of heart disease in your family? Do you smoke? These are just a few of the questions. The answers to these questions and the results of various medical tests can give the medical practitioner an idea of the patient's susceptibility to serious heart or other organic problems.

If body chemistry changes with exercise in both depressed and nondepressed people and if this change is what helps improve the mood of the depressed person, would this change help prevent depression? I do not know the answer, and at this point I can't find anyone who does know.

The above dissertation is a long route to a point I wish to make about the group of people I believe is the most susceptible to serious depression. The words *tension* and *stress* always surround the word *depression* when one tries to explain depression as an environmentally induced disorder. These two words, *tension* and *stress,* bring to mind men working at a busy trading desk in New York or some other money center, or the air traffic controllers landing airliners every three to five minutes, or even a high-school teacher confronting an unruly classroom. These are just TV images; the really stressful situation in our society is that endured by the working mother. "A man's work is from sun to sun, a woman's work is never done." is a phrase that should have been invented for these women. Their home and family problems often invade the workplace, and these problems may have to be solved at work, if humanly possible. Without statistics to back my claim, I'll bet this is now the single largest group that is being diagnosed as clinically depressed.

If exercise were absolutely guaranteed to prevent depression, when in the world would this group of working mothers find the time to participate in any physical activity program? I am not sure how they would find the necessary time because, having been a husband and dad, I always had more free time than my wife. My lack of knowledge of the subject prompted me to interview some fifteen working mothers who exercise regularly and ask how they each found the time. Some of the answers were astounding, but the best came from Sue, a friend, who simply replied, "Short hair and short fingernails." I still don't entirely believe her, but she never changed her story. Another working mother, Deborah, replied that she found time by explaining to her husband that she needed three hours a week, plus travel time, to stay sane. Her time and their schedule were worked out with his assistance once the situation was explained in those terms. Martha, also a working mother, explained to her boss that she needed to attend aerobic classes twice a week and leave work early on those days. When he asked why, Martha replied, "To keep me halfway sane." His next questions were, "Is the cost covered under our insurance plan? Are two days enough?" Barbara found that a church near her home had an aerobic class schedule that coincided with a youth play period. Three days a week, this organization had something for her two-, four-, and five-year-old children. Phyllis, a single parent, persuaded her daughter to ride her bike along with her while she walked and jogged. Another Barbara, the most creative of the group, formed the "Sweat and Diaper" club in her neighborhood. After work, the six members and their children met six days a week at a selected house. Three moms would jog and three would babysit on alternate days. Even one husband finally joined in after the dark evenings of winter set in because of his concern about safety.

After talking to many moms, I concluded that for working mothers to find time to exercise is extremely difficult, sometimes virtually impossible, but when the time is found and used, it does wonders not only for the mom but for the entire family as well.

A FEW REMARKS FROM A COUNTRY AND WESTERN SINGER

The evening I typed what I believed to be the last page of this manuscript I turned the computer off, packed my briefcase, and headed to my favorite country and western club. There I expected to see Billy Bob Roy, a local cowboy singer and nightclub humorist. It was one of his nights to entertain, and as I worked my way to a small table near the stage, he held his hands up and open in a greeting that questioned, "Where have you been lately, Old Goat?"

At intermission he came by the table and asked the same question, as though his fans were expected to frequent his show at least once a week. I told my friend that I had been working on a book each evening after work and, therefore, missed several of my weekly visits to his performance. Of course he asked the title and substance of the book, so I briefly described the contents. To my surprise the little singer began talking. To quote Billy Bob,

> I always thought my depression was caused by that curly-haired woman I was married to. I guess my psychiatrist thought so too, because when I complained about her spending habits and her constant nagging about wanting me to do more so that she could spend more, he, my doctor, never argued or commented. Back then I thought he agreed; now I know he didn't. It never dawned on me that my low-down feelings came from inside and not from the nagging that woman did. Looking back, I guess I would have nagged too, because I never got home till well after the club closed and then I had little to say except good night. When Curly, my wife, finally kicked me out of the house, I had lots of free time because my

work starts at 9:00 at night and goes on till either midnight or two in the morning. Every afternoon was free so I decided to start lifting weights because, at forty-four, I was beginning to get a little beer gut. Rolls around the middle just don't look right on a skinny country and western singer. I asked my psychiatrist about weightlifting and he urged me to get started. It took months to get rid of that little belly and I had to quit having drinks with the customers. Hell, that might have done as much good as the exercise, for all I know.

When I got into that exercise thing I got pretty strong for a little skinny fellow, and I finally began to enjoy it. At first I sure didn't enjoy it, but I was determined that my shirts wouldn't tug at the buttons around my middle.

With the new energy I found, I went out and got a second job. I now sing at happy hour from 5:00 to 7:00, four evenings a week, at one of them yuppie clubs here in town. You have to sing ballads and folk songs for yuppies because they pretend not to like country and western, but I quickly learned new numbers. Once in a while I sing out at the old folks' home for free. The old folks always clap the loudest and the longest because they ain't all hunkered down over their drinks pretending to be solving the world's problems. Speaking of problems, I used to worry about not ever getting a recording contract, no matter how hard I tried. The doctor called it part of my anxiety and gave me pills for that too. I don't fret about that much anymore because I've decided that folks have to come see me to enjoy my performance. I don't know what they think they are seeing because Curly used to tell me that I looked like an organ grinder's monkey all dressed up in blue jeans, boots, and a Stetson. I sort of agree with her, but folks do like my singing. I even quit worrying about looking like the organ grinder's monkey since that beer belly went away.

You know, I guess Curly did me a favor when she kicked me out of the house because I couldn't get much lower down than I was then. By the way, she came by to hear me sing during happy hour a couple of days ago. She said that I acted different and that I was sure packing 'em in. Coming from old Curly, that made me feel real good.

I still see the shrink once a week, 'cause I know there is other stuff I need to get straightened out. I don't think he's working on depression anymore because I sure don't feel like I did a year ago or even six months ago. I do still worry when I think about being forty-four and all I know how to do is play the guitar and sing. I guess folks in other lines of work have that same worry.

You know, I fought that queer low-down feeling, on and off, for five or six years. If I had known a little sweat and a little straining could have saved those years, I sure as hell would have started earlier. For a little guitar-playing organ grinder's monkey, I'm doing a lot better.

Later, while driving home, I wondered if Billy Bob should not have been the co-author of *Defeating Depression*. He said everything that needs to be said in a few hundred words. I bet the talented little guy puts it to music and sings it as a ballad to the yuppies.

STRUCTURING YOUR PROGRAM

People often ask, "What is the best form of exercise?" The answer is, "The form you will do." Physical activity or exercise need not be a complete bore even for those people who detest getting hot and sweaty. These people may never find physical activity as exciting as an expense-paid trip around the world, but it need not be like a daily trip to the dentist. The object is to discover at least two forms of physical activity that you will enjoy and do on a continuing basis. The contents of this section cannot make you an expert in any particular field such as jogging, swimming, cycling, or cross-country skiing. I hope only to introduce you to a few forms of activity and show you how to begin and how to get more involved with those people in your local area who can help you and make the effort an enjoyable one.

Most people who participate in a particular physical activity on a regular basis love to talk about it. Use this built-in love affair to gain knowledge by simply asking a question or two. You will find that most participants will often tell you more than you want to know.

When I first joined a gym, I was impressed by the fact that most of its members looked as if they did not need to be there. This was a busy gym in the downtown area of a large metropolitan center; therefore, it attracted a wide variety of members. In spite of this, everyone except me looked absolutely fit. It was some weeks before I discovered another fat person using the facility, and secretly I was happy to see him there. The other participants, except for me and the other fat guy, fell into three categories. Each category was intimidating. The power lifters, those who could lift two to four hundred pounds with pure muscle and many grunts and groans, made up the first intimidating group. These guys all gathered in a small corner of the gym and coached each other. In dress clothes they might appear fat, because they all had a middle girth of forty or fifty inches, a neck larger than the average thigh, and a huge chest. It was then, and is now, amazing to see the weight these guys could lift, even though I did not then know the names of the different lifts or the difficulty of each.

The next most intimidating group was the bodybuilders. This group, male and female, had muscles that I did not know existed. These rare muscles, as well as the normal muscles, were always visible even when they weren't picking up something or flexing. Here again I was amazed. These men and women have back muscles; thigh muscles, front and back; calf muscles; chest muscles; arm muscles; even butt muscles. They can simply walk to the water fountain and everything flexes. They look so good that I wondered if it might not be uncomfortable to be built like that. This group makes the Greek gods that pass me on the jogging trail look puny.

Then there is the gorgeous female group. They really don't need to exercise because they are perfect. They are thin, perfectly proportioned, have visible muscles only where they look good, but not too many, and they are not too big. These graceful women don't have to walk from machine to machine to exercise, the floor seems to move beneath their feet. All are so flexible that their stretching, before weight training, resembles a Balanchine ballet.

Well, here I was, the Old Goat, fifty-five, overweight, out of shape, and following this group of superhumans from machine to machine. Things were further complicated by the fact that the gym had recently installed new machines that I had never seen, and the print was so small on the instruction placard that I could not read it. One day while desperately confronting one of the new machines, I mumbled to myself, "Somebody please help." Three of the superhumans immediately responded, showed me how to use the machine properly, gave encouragement, and said, "Always ask one of us if you have a problem." That day I learned that my best source of information was the people I was working out with, and they really were not intimidating. Ask questions, without abusing the privilege. You will learn a lot.

After I discovered that the superhumans at the gym were helpful and not really intimidating, as I had thought, I approached one of the Greek gods at the rest area near the jogging trail and asked what I could do to help cure a constantly sore hamstring muscle. His advice, freely given, matched exactly that prescribed by my doctor the week before, so I began to follow it.

I hope this brief narrative of my experience will help you. The people you meet at the gym, your new playmates, for the most part will be nice, helpful people.

The object now is to find a type of aerobic activity that you will enjoy and do. The strength-training segment of your exercise program is limited to weight training using either free weights or machines or both. As mentioned earlier, if neither machines nor weights are available, review the section on strength training at home, which tells you how to use everyday objects and your own body weight to accomplish the same goals.

The first step in the aerobic area is walking, and the second is walking and jogging. Why not walking and swimming? Why not walking and rowing or swimming and cycling? All are fine—just choose any combination that suits you. I have found that a good way to choose is to think back to those things you enjoyed as a child. Was it skating? Was it cycling? Was it swimming? Would you now have the time to do it? Would it be enjoyable again? If your favorite childhood pastime was stamp collecting, we may have a problem unless you would agree to jog to and from the stamp emporium. Croquet can be made aerobic if you agree to run around the court before and after each of your turns. All teasing aside, I truly believe from personal experience that the combination of aerobic and strength training is the most effective therapeutic method for alleviating depression. I hope to help you find the right combination of these two forms of training.

The following brief descriptions of several forms of exercise are written for those people who have never been exposed to or participated in sports or exercise. You may already have an activity in mind and be highly proficient at it. If this is the case, reading the remainder of this book may only suggest an additional activity for you.

HEART RATE

How Fast Should I Run the Engine?

In an earlier section I promised information about measuring and controlling your heart rate during training. Regulating your heart rate to the proper zone can make your physical activity more rewarding and increase your endurance more effectively. The heart-rate level is closely monitored by competing athletes during their training. It is interesting, however, that when physical activity is used as a therapeutic tool for alleviating depression, the heart rate may not be a determining factor for the effectiveness of the treatment. My clue for this assumption is that both anaerobic activities such as weightlifting and aerobic activities such as running and swimming have the same curative effect on those suffering from depression. This being the case, why should one be concerned about training in any particular heart-rate zone or beats per minute? Why not be concerned more with consistency than with exact beats per minute? Earlier I stated my belief that consistency is by far the most important factor in your physical activity program, even to the point that I recommend some physical activity each of the seven days per week. Having said this, I believe some knowledge of what your engine (your heart) is doing for you and what you are doing to it will be enjoyable and helpful in your physical activity program. You can use a widely accepted formula that applies to approximately sixty percent of the population to determine your maximum heart rate or beats per minute. It is your age—your correct age in years—subtracted from 220. In my case it is 46—whoops 56—subtracted from 220. The correct, no-fib result is 164 beats per minute as my maximum rate. My training zones vary downward from this maximum number. You can take your own heart rate on your wrist or neck for ten seconds and multiply times six for your beats per minute, or do as many now do and buy a heart-rate monitor.

The five training zones are well described in a book by Sally Edwards titled *The Heart Rate Monitor Book.* They are summarized below.

1. The Fat-Burning Zone is fifty to sixty percent of your maximum heart rate. In this zone your body will be burning more fat calories than carbohydrates. It is your most relaxed state and is most associated with long, slow distance training. To find your range use the following equation:

Your maximum heart rate of ___ × 0.50 = ___ beats per minute.

Your maximum heart rate of ___ × 0.60 = ___ beats per minute.

If you are among the sixty percent of people who have average hearts that run at average speed, your fat-burning zone would be between these two numbers.

2. The Healthy Heart Zone is from sixty to seventy percent of your maximum heart rate. This zone, referred to as the "aerobic fitness threshold," will begin to benefit your cardiovascular (heart and circulatory) system. To reap total benefit, you should maintain your heart rate at this level for at least 20 minutes. To figure this range, use the previous equation but substitute 0.60 for 0.50 and 0.70 for 0.60.

3. The Aerobic Zone is between seventy and eighty percent of your maximum heart rate. In this zone, you are not only working your cardiovascular system but also your respiratory system. Training that occurs in this range will put more demands on your heart and lungs and cause you to become fitter, faster, and stronger. To figure this range, substitute 0.70 and 0.80 for 0.50 and 0.60, respectively.

4. The Anaerobic Threshold Zone is between eighty and ninety percent of your maximum heart rate. In this zone, you begin to cross over into anaerobic training. Using this type of training will enable your body to metabolize lactic acid much more efficiently. This zone should be used for high-performance training and by experienced athletes. To figure this range, substitute 0.80 and 0.90 for 0.50 and 0.60, respectively.

5. The Red Line Zone is between ninety and one hundred percent. This zone is recommended only for those in extremely fit condition. It is not for the weekend athlete. Entering into this zone will cause you to go into oxygen debt and will mean you have crossed over the anaerobic threshold. This type of training should be used only by those interested in reaching the highest levels of performance.

Now that you know about the five zones of aerobic training, why not try to use this knowledge as it relates to your physical activity program? Zone 1—Fat-Burning—is probably where you will begin your walking program. I have strongly recommended a good brisk walk for at least thirty minutes a day, twice a day if time allows. This zone, fifty to sixty percent of your maximum heart rate, offers you two major benefits. It is your personal beginning point—and what better name could be hoped for than the Fat-Burning Zone. I hope you will, in the months to come, pass through the Healthy Heart Zone and settle in toward the top of Zone 3, the Aerobic Zone, that is, at about eighty percent of your maximum heart rate. All the zones will have the same therapeutic effect, but as noted by Sally Edwards, working out in Zone 3 will cause you to become fitter, stronger, and faster. You were warned that the side effects of this program would be good.

Earlier in this section, I stated that these ranges would probably fit sixty percent of the population—those who have average hearts. Some folks have unusually slow heart rates, and some have unusually fast heart rates. Such conditions are neither good nor bad, just a little different. I see them the way I see two types of windmills.

You have probably seen the country windmill, which is about thirty feet tall with blades constructed of sheet metal. Each blade is about thirty-six inches long. With sufficient wind, the blades spin so fast that they become blurred. Contrast this with the Dutch windmill, which is three stories tall, with the blades spanning from a point above the top of the structure to a point only a few feet above the ground. The blades are about thirty-five feet long. Both windmills pump water, and they may even pump the same amount of water, but they perform these tasks differently.

Covert Bailey, the author of *Fit or Fat in America*, stated in one of his TV programs that fifty percent of the people could, and do, use common sense when it comes to the intensity of exercise. Women seem to make up the entire fifty percent. Men, too often, are overcome by the "macho hormone" and overdo physical activity quickly. A word to the men: Take it slow. Move up to the different heart-rate zones over time. Don't try to get to Zones 4 and 5 after only a week or two. Be patient and consistent.

A common sense method of judging your heart rate when exercising is talking aloud. One can do this when jogging, biking, walking, or rowing, but not when swimming, of course. While exercising, recite "Mary had a little lamb. Its fleece was white as snow. Everywhere that Mary went the lamb was sure to go." If you can recite this first verse of my favorite nursery rhyme without a breath, you are not trying hard enough. Pick it up a little. If you are macho, it might be a good idea to pick another poem or verse. The guy next to you may not believe you are really macho if he overhears you saying "Mary had a little lamb" too often.

WALKING

What an easy and enjoyable way to start a physical activity program, and everyone already knows how! We walk some at work; we walk to shop, walk to and from our automobile, walk up ramps at football games, and so on. Most of this walking is over a distance of one or two hundred yards at any one time. For the next few weeks you will be expected to walk at least thirty minutes at a time if that is your endurance limit or a full hour if you can easily accomplish that much continuous walking. Continuous walking presents a few more problems than the short walks we do daily.

First, your shoes absolutely have to fit and they need to be designed for walking or running. Your feet may be tender and will need time to toughen up. It is a good idea to rub a lubricant between your toes, at least during the first week or so. Many runners do this every time they run, so it may be a practice that you want to continue. Your toes can rub together and become sore even though blisters may not form. Wear socks that will allow moisture to pass through them—use cotton socks in the summer and wool socks when it is really cold. Your feet need tender loving care in the beginning because you will be walking two to four miles a day. Keep your feet happy!

Drink two large glasses of water or sports drink two hours before you plan to walk. You need to do this in both warm and cold months because you will perspire no matter what the weather is. If it is hot and if you are not used to outdoor activity, consider carrying a full water bottle with you. Proper hydration is important, so drink more fluids than you think you need and drink *before* you become thirsty.

Buy and wear proper clothing for the climate, and do not forget sunscreen, which is important from the beginning. Sunscreens now available are impervious to perspiration. Men carry a sweat rag; women seem to prefer a perspiration cloth—same rag, different name.

Now that you are properly prepared, once again pledge to be nice to your feet, select your route, and go.

Most people can walk a mile in about fifteen or sixteen minutes. Thus a thirty-minute walk would cover about two miles; a one-hour walk about four miles. Do not be concerned about distance at this point; consider only time. Part of the object in walking a continuous thirty minutes is to move your heart rate up to fifty to sixty percent of your maximum rate and to keep it there for at least twenty of the thirty minutes walked. If you have had little or no physical activity for some time, a brisk walk will accomplish this goal.

My experience has convinced me that I feel better mentally after walking a full hour than I do if I am able to squeeze in only thirty minutes. If you are fit enough to walk an hour, do so as soon as possible. If not, start at the lower level and work toward the day when you can. I suspect that a long, brisk walk makes even a well-trained athlete feel a little better mentally. A few months ago I walked my favorite six-mile loop with a young triathlete because we had something to discuss. Certainly this activity caused no strain on this person because she trains to swim two miles and to cycle forty-eight miles. She finishes with a ten-mile run. However, when we finished the walk, she smiled and commented, "That was sort of fun."

The next section is on walking and jogging. If you believe—or know—that you are unfit, stay with the walk. Make it your only routine for a reasonable time, until you're ready for more.

WALK/JOG

This exercise program, which I call the walk/jog, may help you attain rapid increases in your cardiovascular function. Up to this point, your walking has strengthened your leg and back muscles, and if done properly, it has increased your heart rate above the resting rate to fifty to sixty percent of your maximum heart rate.

If you were in poor physical condition when you started the walking program, the introduction of the walk/jog program has to be done carefully. Do not overdo it. Do not start by setting a goal of walking for half a mile and jogging for half a mile. The initial goal of this program is to increase your heart rate up to sixty to seventy percent of your maximum rate and keep it there for at least part of the time you have allotted to walking. If you have been walking thirty minutes at a time, or about two miles, you should now walk/jog the same amount of time. This will increase your distance slightly. You will have to experiment during your walking period to see how long and how far you are capable of jogging. Again, do not attempt to walk half the distance and run half. Initially, the running segments should be a minute or two in duration. Walk two minutes, then jog two minutes. These segments do not have to be perfectly timed.

The jogging sections are designed to raise your heart rate above that attained when walking. The walking sections are designed to let you catch your breath and let your heart rate return almost to the rate you attain during your normal walking period. Try to make sure that your walking periods are not so long that your heart rate falls to that of a normal walk. The purpose is really twofold. You want to begin to use your heart muscles more vigorously and your leg and back muscles more intensely. Try to get sufficient rest when walking so that you are not gasping for breath, but keep your internal engine—your heart—running at a fairly good pace. Once you have caught your breath during the walk, run again at a slow pace until you feel out of breath again. Repeat this routine over and over until you have used your allotted exercise time.

Remember to start slowly and progress slowly. Do not get macho and try to push too far or run too fast. Do not try to keep up with other runners, and do not worry about who passes you. That you are running short distances and then walking when other joggers are running the same or longer distances should be of no concern. Don't worry about the fact that you are out of breath and sound like an old steam engine while some runners pass you and are able to talk in a normal voice. Your time will come, but it does take time to get in good physical condition. As I have said time and time again, this exercise program is doing good things for your mental health right now. The physical conditioning that will result is only a positive side effect—not your primary concern.

Running puts much more stress on your body, especially your feet, ankles, knees, hips, and back muscles, than walking does. If something hurts, stop and walk. Do not try to run through a pain or run with a pain.

Repeat the pledge to be loving and kind to your feet by wearing properly designed and fitted shoes. Drink sufficient water or sports drink before and during your walk/jog period, use sunscreen if needed, wear clothes that allow perspiration to evaporate, and use some common sense about how you feel. Again, do not overdo it; the time you spend in the walk/jog program should be enjoyable. If you push too hard, it will not be enjoyable. If you walk/jog at a reasonable pace and on a consistent basis, the walk/jog program will produce positive changes in your endurance. You won't be gasping for breath near the end of your running period. Your heart rate will decline (reach its recovery rate) faster when you begin to walk. You will be able to jog longer distances or more minutes at a time. The pace of your jogging and walking will pick up. You need not measure these results, but they will be there.

Two pieces of sports equipment may help you with this program: one is a sports watch (stop watch), and the other is a sports heart monitor. Because I am a gadget buyer, I own both. I use the watch to time the length of my running periods, and at one time I thought the heart monitor was very important. However, I found that you can judge your internal heart rate by the way you feel and by your breathing rate. Besides, I am not training to enter some competitive event. My engineer friends seem to really like these gadgets, and they keep intricate records of their progress. Recently I read of a heart monitor that can plug into your personal computer, download your training information as to time, date, duration, and heart rate, and produce a colored graph that shows your progress. That is a heck of a deal, but I haven't even mastered the VCR at this point, so I'd better pass.

People often ask, "How long should I stay with the walking program? How many weeks should I walk/jog before I run the full route?" There is no set answer to these questions. It depends on how you feel and how the physical activity makes you feel. I made the assumption that most depressed people are sedentary and physically unfit; therefore, walking is the logical place to start. The next logical step is the walk/jog, and the next step is running. You may never progress to the running stage because you might discover another aerobic activity that is more enjoyable or more convenient. Perhaps running or even the walk/jog program is out of the question for you because of a physical injury or handicap. It is my feeling that a physical activity program intended to combat the symptoms of unipolar depression needs to be reasonably strenuous, consistent, and aerobic on some days and should contain an element of strength training on other days. If these prerequisites are met, I do not believe the progression in your program to the next level need be of concern. If walking four days a week and weight training three days do the trick, and if you have no desire to progress further, that's fine. Just stay with it. Above all else, stay with it.

CYCLING

A few years back, and close to one of my birthdays, my daughter asked what I would like as a present. Without really thinking about it, I replied, "A bicycle, if one can be found like I had as a kid." The image

I had in mind was a balloon-tired, single-speed, coaster-brake, steel-framed machine, kickstand and all—the same heavy-duty bike that all kids had in the late forties and early fifties. Several days later my daughter reported that after visiting several bike shops she had concluded that the type of bike I had described was no longer manufactured or certainly not available in our city. In its place, I then suggested the standard generic birthday gift for all fathers, a white dress shirt and tie.

Both conversations were forgotten until the morning of my birthday when breakfast was served in bed and a shiny new black bicycle with lots of gears, a French name I couldn't pronounce, hand brakes, and some kind of shifting levers on the handle bars was presented. The only resemblance to my old-time bike was the balloon or, "fat" tires as they are now called. I was grateful for, but also confused and astounded by, this complicated machine, though I figured that if my teenage children could ride one of these things, I certainly could.

After finishing breakfast and before leaving on my experimental ride, I was informed that this machine was a mountain bike, and I learned to pronounce the name. We live on the flat plains of Texas, so the only mountains we see are in the movies, but I had a true mountain bike, gears and all. My experimental ride was successful enough, when you consider that I now had to stop with hand brakes, not by pushing backward on the pedals. And out of twenty-one different gear combinations, I had to find a ratio that felt like my old-time bike. There is no longer a chain guard, so my pants leg immediately got caught in the chain. After a few evening rides, I caught on to all the gadgets and found that this newfangled mountain bike was a fun machine to ride. It was a good thing that our neighborhood has no mountains, or even hills, because about the best I could accomplish in a one-hour evening ride was eleven miles, according to my new high-tech speedometer.

As it turned out, my intelligent children had made a wise choice of equipment for an old bike rider like me, who was "born again"— starting over from childhood. When you consider cycling as a form of physical activity, your choice of equipment will be equally important. If, however, one has an old bike hanging in the garage or stored elsewhere, air up the tires, have it safety-checked, and start with it. Beginning is the most important accomplishment, and the proper equipment can evolve over time.

I continued with the evening neighborhood rides and, at times, rode fair distances in the country. While riding in the country, I became accustomed to the young Turks passing me in the blink of an eye. What became annoying, however, was that older, heavier, and less-conditioned people were also passing me on their skinny-tired road bikes. Well, I had to have one of those faster things. But I could not wait the nine months until my next birthday, and the next birthday would surely be the year of the shirt and tie once again, anyway. The following weekend, I bought a new touring road bike with clip-on pedals and all the accouterments. The complete package cost more than my first automobile, but now I could at least keep up with the other old folks. The young Turks will always be there to annoy and to be envied.

Have you learned more about cycling equipment? I hope so. There are road bikes where the rider leans forward onto the drop handlebars with his/her rear end perched high on a skinny little saddle (seat). Such bikes have thin tires, hand brakes, and fourteen to twenty-one gears and are lightweight. My first machine—a mountain, or all-terrain, bike—has fat tires. The rider sits erect and grips straight handlebars. It has twenty-one gears and often has knobby tires for traction on sand or dirt surfaces. A third type of bicycle, the hybrid, a cross of the two bikes already described, has somewhat narrow tires, straight handlebars, all the gears, and so on. Your selection of equipment should be predicated on the type of riding you plan to do in your particular area. Ask more than a few local bikers if in doubt. It's not un-American to own two bikes, so don't overlook that possibility.

Cycling as a form of exercise is more difficult to accomplish logistically than walking or jogging might be, especially if you live in an urban area and have to contend with automobile traffic. Once into it, you will find that it is worth the effort, even though most city dwellers are required to transport their bikes by automobile into the country for a safe and enjoyable ride.

Because of the mechanical advantage inherent in all bikes, an hour of cycling, especially on flat terrain, does not expend nearly the amount of energy that an hour spent jogging does. I have seen various ratings for comparing biking with running, walking, and even swimming. If you are interested in deriving your own "homemade" ratio, try biking for ten minutes at a good clip, then rest for twenty minutes, and finally jog for ten minutes. Did you expend five times as much energy jogging? Three times as much? Work out your own ratio, but remember that cycling requires more time to accomplish your exercise goal.

It is true that one never forgets how to ride a bike, but remember how to start again safely—wear a helmet and do not ride after dark.

All cities and most towns have at least one cycling club, and all cycling clubs want new members. Inquire at a bike shop about the type of riders that make up the membership. Some cycling clubs are strictly for racers (young Turks), while others cater to a wider segment of the cycling public. Don't prejudge the membership by the club name. In my town, Greased Lightning Saddle Tramps is composed of anyone above fifty years of age who can still stand. Cycling has grown so popular that it is easy to find riders at your skill level. Call a club, join it, and attend both their meetings and their rides.

DURATION AND INTENSITY

Although considerations of duration and intensity apply to all exercise activities, I decided to discuss these issues in the context of cycling because virtually everyone has ridden a bike, if only in childhood, and because cycling presents a much wider range of intensity and duration than virtually any other activity. As a kid, do you remember racing someone on your bike? It was not an organized race, but one in which you were challenged, or you may have challenged someone else, to see who would be first to get from here to there. From the time of the challenge until you crossed the chosen finish line, both you and your opponent exerted all the strength and energy possible to win. At the finish line both of you were out of breath, your legs probably ached, and you were happy to step off your bike. This, of course, was a form of intense physical activity. As a child, you probably called it fun. On the other hand, if one day you rode leisurely to school, found it to be a holiday, then rode around an hour or so before returning home, this longer-than-usual ride might be an example of duration. You may have expended the same amount of energy on each ride, the first like a sprinter and the second like a distance runner on a slow, leisurely training run. Keep in mind that what might be intense to the beginning exerciser would probably be a leisurely walk in the park to the trained athlete. I believe that duration has much to do with the curative effects of physical activity on depression. I believe it is better to walk for an hour than run hard for five minutes. It is better to bike for two hours than to strenuously lift weights for fifteen minutes. There is no scientific proof of this; it is simply something I have experienced. For the beginner in most physical activity programs, duration may be difficult to accomplish. For the out-of-shape beginner, it would be virtually impossible to run or swim for an hour. Not so with walking and cycling. Although other activities probably offer this advantage, I am sure of walking and cycling because I use them as my duration exercises.

As a "born-again" cyclist, which most of us are who rode as youngsters, you will be surprised how substantially your mileage can increase with very little riding time. A fifty-mile ride may seem out of the question at first, but in a few months it will be fun—if only a few precautions are taken in those first few months.

1. Don't try to keep up with a stronger, more experienced rider your first few times out. If riding with a stronger rider, have the route planned, and possibly even a map of the route, and agree to meet back at the starting point so that each cyclist can ride at his/her own pace.

2. Give your legs, and especially your bottom, time to toughen up. This in itself could take several months if you are able to ride only on weekends.

3. Don't initially choose courses that are too long. Remember you have to get there and back, and the wind always seems to be against you on the way home. If you have a map, know the escape routes, or shorter ways, back to the start.

4. Don't push for twelve or fifteen miles between rest stops when it would be more enjoyable to stop every eight or ten.

5. Don't worry about being the last one to finish. Do stop to smell the flowers. Never pass a country bakery or ice cream shop without stopping. The owners need the business. It is your duty to stop, and all country-consumed calories have been scientifically proved to burn up in the next two miles ridden.

SWIMMING

Born-again swimmers are not as common as born-again bikers, and there are reasons for this. Swimming requires skills that may have declined sharply or been lost after a period of disuse. Or perhaps the skills were never very good. In any case, the need to relearn skills or perhaps to learn them for the first time does not mean that swimming should be overlooked as a recreational form of exercise. Swimming has so many advantages that it should be vigorously pursued and the necessary skills learned or relearned.

When one states that swimming has advantages over other forms of physical activity, the obvious and often-stated phrase comes to mind: "Swimming exercises the whole body." True enough—it probably does. But consider some of the other advantages. Swimming can be pursued in the blistering heat of summer, when the heat and humidity may preclude most other forms of outdoor activity. And swimming makes you feel good from head to toe. If a heated indoor pool is available, swimming can be practiced in the dead of winter when it is too cold and miserable to be outside. Swimming can be accomplished with several different strokes, some of which do not require timed and skillful breathing. Finally, learning again or learning for the first time and the practice involved probably produce the therapeutic effect one hopes to find in exercise. This list of advantages should convince you that swimming ought to be included in your program as soon as is practical.

I have found that good adult swim instructors are not as plentiful as good beginning instructors for children. This observation stands to reason when one considers that most beginning swimmers are children so most instructors have more experience teaching these first-time young learners. Good adult classes are available, however, for both true beginners and adult intermediates. Do your searching through the local YMCA, the Red Cross, and private health and fitness clubs.

I recently asked an excellent and experienced adult instructor what type of people made up the majority of her classes. She explained, "Age thirty-five to fifty, a few older. Most are somewhat afraid of the water, but they want to step out there and learn, although they remain cautious for a while. They are fearful but not overwhelmingly fearful. This apprehension may be rooted in the fact that big brother held their head beneath the water once, or once too often, or maybe they grew up with no access to the water or swimming pools—you know, the desert." She continued to explain that when adult beginners master a particular technique or accomplish a particular goal, they become more excited than the children. The children never knew that they couldn't do it, but the adults know that just weeks ago they could not swim the length of the pool, no matter what stroke they used.

If some or all of this description sounds familiar, you may as well find an adult beginner's or intermediate class and sign up. You will probably fit right in.

Because I had now found an excellent source of information, I continued to question this young instructor. She mentioned that it would be a good idea to tell the instructor you find that your goal is to use swimming as a form of exercise. You want to learn to swim for a twelve-minute time duration and someday reach twenty minutes. Explain your goal, because your individual goal is somewhat different from that of the person who just bought a new boat, cannot swim, and does not want to go down with the ship.

Next, I queried, "What if you are a person who learned to swim as a child, has no access to adult swimming classes, cannot find a private tutor, but does want to swim for exercise?" I admit I had posed an unlikely scenario, but her answer was rather interesting. "We have three basic strokes. The easiest to master for the purpose of exercise is the breaststroke because the timing of one's breathing is not a factor. The swimmer's head is almost completely out of the water and by just lifting the chin slightly breathing can be accomplished. It is not that difficult to swim twelve minutes using the breaststroke, even for the born-again swimmer who is out of shape. Like the walk/jog program, it is okay to stop at the end of the pool, hold on to the side, and catch your breath. The continuous twelve- or even twenty-minute swim will eventually evolve. The next stroke I would use for exercise, if one finds free-style difficult, is the elementary backstroke. Elementary means that the swimmer's arms do not pass his shoulders, and the arms are drawn back up to the shoulder line beneath the water. Breathing is not obstructed because you are swimming on your back. Both of these strokes are fun. The swimmer can alternate the two and get quite a bit of exercise."

"Why is free-style so difficult?" I asked. "That is what I learned at five years of age."

My instructor friend replied, "It is not difficult; there are simply more separate movements to be learned—three, in fact—and they must all fit together if you want to become an accomplished swimmer. One needs to learn the proper position of the body in the water, the proper arm stroke and kick, and controlled breathing. Before leaving the breaststroke, you might think about the fact that people who have never been taught free-style, which was once called the Australian crawl, seem to use the breaststroke rather naturally. Films made in the South Pacific show natives using the breaststroke. They swim to travel from place to place in the water, and their heads are partly out of the water for breathing and sight. The speed is not as fast as free-style, but they probably are not in a hurry anyway. If I were a South Pacific native, I would not be in a hurry. I don't want anyone to think the breaststroke is a sissy way of swimming, or not macho, because it is probably the first stroke used by our ancestors to cross water. I've always wondered how Tarzan learned and then became so accomplished at the free-style method while living in the jungle with Jane and Cheetah. The old movies would have been a fraction more believable if Tarzan had used the breaststroke."

My instructor friend then continued: "During this club's open swim periods, I have seen many people intent on exercise use the breaststroke exclusively and swim much longer than twenty minutes at a time, but you asked about the difficulty in learning free-style. It is a learned stroke and it takes practice. The swimmer's body has to remain parallel with the surface of the water and shallow in the water. Legs are kept parallel by an adequate kick. The head should not drift downward; therefore, it is better if the swimmer looks at the wall with the surface of the water hitting him/her at mid forehead. The arm stroke should enter the water in front of shoulders and at the eleven and one o'clock positions in relationship to the head. The kick, done with a slightly bent leg and toes pointed, should extend twelve to eighteen inches beneath the water but not break the water surface. Breathing is executed by turning the head to the side and slightly back toward the shoulder. All this is then condensed in a flowing, rhythmic motion to pull the body through the water. Do you see why we don't teach beginners from a book?"

The young lady finished my education by mentioning, "If a person cannot swim, cannot obtain even beginner's lessons, or absolutely has no interest in swimming, water aerobics offers a few of the benefits of swimming. The participant in water aerobics exercise enjoys the good feel of the water, the heart rate is elevated, and many of the body muscles are used against the resistance of the water. It's kind of fun and good for you."

RUN/JOG

Logically, the run/jog section should immediately follow the walk/jog section. However, I inserted the ideas on swimming and cycling to allow everyone a pleasant ride in the country and a cool refreshing dip in the pool. Now it is time to get back to this hot and difficult subject matter.

If you have faithfully followed the instructions contained in the walk/jog section for some months, no doubt you have learned something about your ability to run. All humans do not have the same ability to run or jog because of differences in heart and lung ability and capacity. Virtually all of us can, however, use running as one of the better forms of endurance training. The differences in physical structure, heart and lung capacity, and ability are so great that what I consider an all-out run is a slow monotonous jog to the trained runner. Consider these factors and these differences when you begin to run. Do not press yourself beyond your capabilities.

The initial goal, possibly not attainable in the first few weeks, is to develop the ability to jog continuously for a twenty-minute period. Twenty minutes is not a number pulled out of thin air. This number has reasoning behind it. To maintain cardiovascular condition, you need to use your heart at the level of seventy to eighty percent of its maximum rate for at least twelve minutes, three times per week. A twenty-minute jog will accomplish this goal for most people. From the start of a run, the first four or five minutes are used to elevate one's heart rate from the resting rate up to the seventy to eighty percent level. During the next twelve minutes the heart rate is maintained at this level. The three or four minutes remaining at the end of the run allow the runner time to slow down and finish at a slower and more relaxed running pace and heart rate. Logically, running or jogging for longer periods of time at the seventy to eighty percent heart rate level will increase endurance.

If you were unfit at the beginning, started with the walk program, then progressed to the walk/jog portion, there is no assurance that you can now run for a continuous twenty minutes. Some people will be able to accomplish this running time, and some will not. The twenty-minute run is an intermediate goal, and it should be approached only as a goal, not as a necessity.

Some people will find it easy to jog for twenty minutes, and others will find it difficult. If you are one who finds it easy to jog for twenty minutes, go for it. Then move on to the thirty-minute level. If, on the other hand, it is difficult, jog as long as you can, then walk a short distance before jogging again. This is the flip side of the walk/jog program with the emphasis on running. In this workout period, run as much as you can and walk as little as possible.

Your experience from the walk/jog period should have provided the necessary information on shoe construction and fit, proper clothing, and adequate hydration. The other factor you might now consider is the surface on which you run. If you run along city streets, the only choice is concrete or asphalt. Softer surfaces are better if they can be found. If possible, find a track or jogging trail constructed with an artificial surface designed for running.

Time, patience, and the ability to stick with it are all required to develop endurance and running skills. Keep this in mind when you begin.

STRENGTH TRAINING

The scientific studies reviewed in the appendix relate that strength training has the same positive effect on the mood of depressed individuals as aerobic activity.

Improvement in your self-concept is an important additional mental benefit of strength training when compared with aerobic training alone. These two factors should be sufficiently compelling to induce anyone suffering from depression to participate in a strength-training or a weight-lifting program. When you couple the mental benefits with the physical benefits, you may feel compelled to include strength training as part of your multiprong therapeutic program.

We have learned about the mental benefits, so now consider the physical benefits. Muscle is ten times more metabolically active than fat. In plain English that means that one pound of lean muscle burns ten times the food fuel as does one pound of fat. This tenfold increased requirement and consumption of simple and complex sugars by the muscle tissue over that required by fatty tissue remains constant regardless of your activity level. Muscle tissue requires more fuel than fatty tissue whether you are resting or physically active. Once strength training has developed these lean muscles, any activity you do will require and use more fuel. We measure this conversion of food into energy and heat as calories. A popular phrase of the day is "burning calories." If you want to produce a more efficient calorie burner, build some lean muscles.

Your metabolic rate—the rate at which your body converts food combined with oxygen into energy and heat—increases after physical activity. The physical activity can be either strength training or aerobic activity, although aerobic activity is the most effective method of increasing your metabolic rate. This increase in metabolic rate is the true cause of weight loss.

Weight training and aerobic activity both have a hand in the pleasant phenomenon of losing weight. A simplified, nontechnical view of one's increased metabolic rate can be visualized if you imagine a thermometer-type instrument marked in degrees from ten to one hundred. As you sit at your desk on a slow workday, your metabolic rate may be slightly below fifty degrees on the measuring stick. At lunch you work out with weight machines for an hour and then return to the sitting job at your office. During the workout your metabolic rate could rise to the ninety degree level, but back at work, and again sitting, you may find that it remains around the seventy degree level for two or three hours. This continued high metabolic rate is a good side effect of weight training or aerobic activity, and it is the way weight is lost. Many people have the misconception that one has to exercise long enough and hard enough to cause the body to burn all the simple and complex sugars in its supply, at which point the body will throw a switch and begin to burn stored fats. In part this is true, but it occurs over a long time, usually months. Even your early physical activity begins to change your metabolic rate. Your strength training is the most efficient method to build lean muscle, which in turn requires and consumes more food energy. In time your body pushes on the switch more gently and a little at a time; thus it begins to use some stored fat as an alternative source of fuel to produce energy. You now require more food energy because you have more muscle tissue to support and feed.

Strength training produces one astonishing result for the beginner. Most newcomers are surprised at how quickly they develop additional muscle strength, measured from their starting point. It is common to observe a newcomer begin his/her first routine with a twenty-pound weight, and in only two months the same person will be using a sixty-pound weight. If one seeks instant gratification, good record keeping will soon show the increased weight results, and these results will be gratifying. Do not, however, push for increased weight alone. It is important to learn the proper and safe form before overtaxing the joints and tendons. Consistency and proper form will allow one to move up in weights without really being conscious of the accomplishment until the workout records are reviewed. Muscle strength develops before weight loss or changes in body contour are evident.

Increased flexibility and greater muscle endurance are additional results of a properly structured and consistent weight-training program. These two by-products will help make your chosen aerobic activity easier and more enjoyable.

Some people build muscle mass easily, and some do not. The predominant determining factor is the body's production of testosterone, the hormone that prompts the body to build muscle mass. If weight training does not prompt your body to produce visible muscle mass, the benefits of strength training are still important. Your muscles will become stronger, leaner, and more flexible, and your muscle endurance will increase.

How does the newcomer start strength training? The simplest method is to go to a health club or gym and ask for instruction. Most health-club employees can convey the basics, show you the proper machines and free weights, demonstrate the safe use of these weights and machines, and outline the starting program. As you progress, questions will, no doubt, arise; they can be answered by these health-club employees.

A good book about strength training will also answer many of your new-found questions. One such book for the female strength trainer is *Body Flex–Body Magic* by Anja Langer, published by Contemporary Books of Chicago. Langer, a woman of German descent, is a professional bodybuilder who started her amateur career in 1980 at the age of fifteen. The first section of her book is written with the newcomer in mind, and the book slowly progresses through advanced-level techniques. Langer includes a section describing the maintenance routines she followed while she was pregnant. This book is also adequate for male beginners in the strength-training game, minus the section on motherhood, of course. Certainly the pictures of this pretty blond woman are more pleasing than those in most weightlifting books I have seen. A good book can answer many questions, and this is one such book.

Strength training can be accomplished at home if you can afford to buy the necessary weights and benches and if you have the floor space needed for this equipment. Much home weight equipment is available, some good and some not so good. Those who choose to train at home generally use free weights as the backbone of their equipment. Free weights require more skill to be used properly, and the learning curve is steeper than that of learning to use the machines found at a gym. Be wary of advertisements that claim "one machine does all," because there are too many muscle groups that need work. Why make your body fit the machine? Find the machine or weights that most efficiently work each group of muscles. As mentioned earlier, strength training can be accomplished without the aid of free weights or weight machines. Marine boot camp has proved this fact. But resistance training, or weight training, is much more efficient and simply more fun in my opinion. If, however, you choose the Marine method, please refer to the next section.

STRENGTH TRAINING AT HOME

If you are of my vintage, you should remember a popular song of the early fifties titled "Dry Bones." The first verse went something like this.

> De toe bone connected to de foot bone
> De foot bone connected to de ankle bone
> De ankle bone connected to de leg bone
> De leg bone connected to de knee bone
> Now hear de word of de Lord.

Chorus:
    Dem bones, dem bones, dem dry bones
    Dem bones, dem bones, dem dry bones
    Dem bones, dem bones, dem dry bones
    Now hear de word of de Lord.

The song continued up through the skeleton, interrupted occasionally for the chorus until it reached the head bone. You can believe it or not, but "Dry Bones" was a popular song for months.

I plan to address strength training by the same method "Dry Bones" used to explain the skeleton—without the chorus, of course. I will use the major muscle groups, not the individual bones that compose the skeleton, and I will start in the middle, not with the toe. Those people who opt to go to a gym or to use free weights and training machines can learn from this section because they will work the same muscle groups but use more complex and more efficient training aids.

Starting in the middle with the tummy muscles—abdominals as they are called—you will need to do two modified types of sit-ups to strengthen these important muscles. The abdominals and the lower back muscles may be the two most important groups for maintaining good conditioning. Besides, like the hip bone in "Dry Bones," the abdominals and lower back muscles hold our two parts, the upper and the lower body, together.

All variations of sit-ups stress and strengthen the *rectus abdominis* muscle wall, and this is what we want. The straight-legged sit-up, where our legs are fully extended and held firmly against the floor, is not what we want. This kind of sit-up can injure the lower back.

The abdominal curl, also called the ab curl, is accomplished by lying flat on your back with your knees up and your feet flat on the floor. Hold your knees slightly forward and apart a few inches. Bring your chin up until it almost touches your chest. In this sit-up variation you will not bring your lower back off the floor; you will raise only your upper back. Fold your hands across your chest and then pull your upper back up toward your knees. At the top of this movement your upper back should be at about a thirty-degree angle to the floor, but the lower back should still be flat on the floor. When you uncurl from the top, or sit-up, position, continue to hold your chin forward and do not let your head touch the floor. The ab curl works your upper abdominals (solar plexus area). Do this exercise at medium speed, and concentrate on the muscles that are pulling. Do not bob up

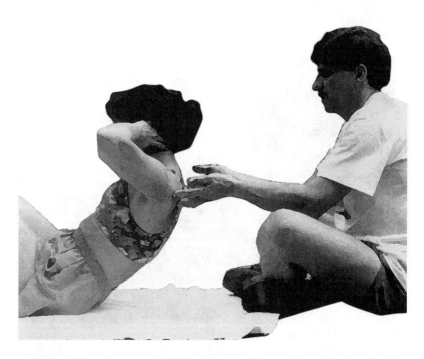

and down. In time you will develop a medium-slow rhythm for this exercise.

Because most of us neglect our tummy muscles, you may be able to do only one, two, or three of these modified sit-ups during the first few days. In time, though, you will be doing ten or more, and it won't take long. These muscles recuperate quickly, making it permissible to work them daily if you choose.

The elbow-knee ab curl works both the lower and upper abdominals. You do it much the same way you do the ab curl, except that you bring your feet off the floor and your knees toward your tummy. Hold your knees in this position and, with your chin tucked forward, lace your fingers behind your head. Now, as before, raise your upper body about thirty degrees with the lower back flat against the floor. Bring your elbows forward and try to touch your legs below your knees. When using this version of the ab curl, always keep your head off the floor and your chin tucked in.

Both of these exercises will be difficult if the abdominal muscles have been neglected. If you can do only one or two, do that number two or three times daily. You have to start somewhere, and soon the numbers and effort will work in your favor. It is possible that some people will be unable to do even one repetition of either of these modified sit-ups. If you are such a person, find an exercise partner and let the partner help you in the following manner until your abdominals become stronger.

Have your partner sit cross-legged on the floor. You lie on the floor on your back with your head on your partner's ankles where they cross. Bring your knees forward, but keep your feet flat on the floor, and again lace your fingers behind your head. The partner places his/her hands behind your shoulders near the shoulder blades. When you begin the sit-up motion, the partner assists by gently pushing on your back. The down movement back to the starting position should be done slowly and with no assistance. Within a few weeks you will

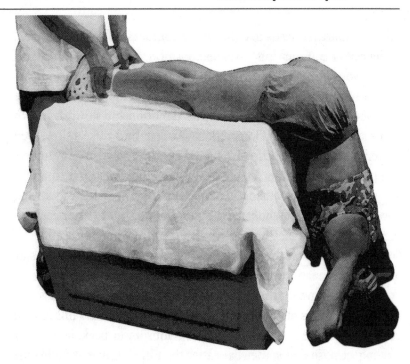

strengthen your abdominal muscles and be able to progress to the more advanced exercises.

Now let's work on the other muscles that help hold our two parts together. These muscles are in the lower back. Two related exercises—the back arch and the inverted sit-up—will strengthen these muscles.

The back arch is executed by lying face down and flat on the floor. Lace your fingers behind your head. Slowly pull your upper body upward, forming an arch with your back. Do not jerk up, and do not bob up. Pull up slowly and let down slowly. You may find that you can raise your chest only a couple of inches from the floor. This distance is fine at the beginning: the distance you can raise your chest will increase as you build lower-back strength. Do not overdo this exercise early in your program. Lower-back muscles are not often used, and sudden overuse can cause soreness. A good starting number for this exercise might be five or six for the first week, then increase to eight or ten.

A variation of this exercise is to have someone hold your feet securely while you lie flat on your stomach on a bed or other elevated flat surface and then let your head and upper body droop over the side. Your partner needs to either sit on your legs or hold them stable in the calf area. From this L-shaped position, again lace your fingers behind your head. Then slowly pull your upper body up to and parallel with your legs. You can then arch your back slightly and go above the level of your legs. Reverse the upward motion and slowly let down to the starting position. Don't jerk your upper body. Use a slow, even movement in both directions. Again, start with five or six movements and progress to eight or ten when you feel ready. Any participant in any physical activity needs strong abdominal muscles and strong lower-back muscles. The exercises described above are not easy for the beginner, but they can be mastered in time and with effort. If your beginning point is two or three movements, do those and stay with it.

Now let's move up the body to the chest and arms. Here the exercise you need to start with is the knee push-up. Because this altered version of push-ups puts little stress on your lower back, it is a safer starting exercise and somewhat easier than the familiar straight-line

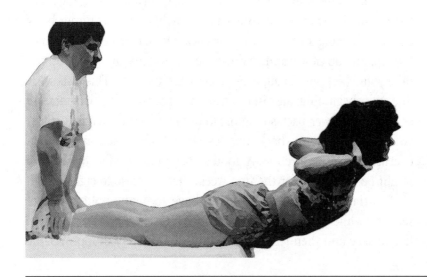

push-up. It works and strengthens your chest muscles below the collar bones (pectoral muscles). It also develops the backs of your upper arms (triceps).

Kneel on the ground and extend your body forward, placing your hands on the ground and slightly farther apart than your shoulders. The wider apart your hands are placed, the more the chest muscles will be worked. With knees remaining on the ground, lower your upper body until your nose brushes the ground. Now, using your arm and chest strength, push straight up to the starting position. Repeat this up-and-down push as many times as is comfortable. If you can do only four or five, rest a while and then attempt that number again before leaving this exercise.

I have seen people who cannot push up once after their chest first touches the ground. In this case one has to do the lowering motion over and over, by slowly lowering the body to the ground, coming to rest chest down on the surface, kneeling back up, and returning to the starting position. A boot-camp drill instructor taught this method to those recruits who had trouble doing the first push-up. I can't use the same language the DI used during his instruction, but using his method with the special class for fifteen minutes a day, twice a day,

everyone learned this important military maneuver before the glori-
ous six-week training period was over. The DI's method takes longer,
but eventually you will be doing a regulation push-up, although of the
knee-touch variety.

To concentrate on the back of your arms, use the same push-up
movement, but bring your elbows in toward and parallel with your
sides. Your hands should be only an inch or two outside your shoulders. This is an isolated exercise to develop the triceps (back upper-
arm muscles).

Chin-ups, or pull-ups, are an excellent exercise for building
strength in the shoulders, chest, arms, and back. A secure chinning bar
is required. You may not have one at home, but you can find these bars
in most parks and along many jogging trails. To develop your chest
muscles, use a bar grip about the width of your shoulders with your
fingers wrapped around the bar toward you. Pull up as many consec-
utive times as possible, rest, and do the pull-ups again. To develop the
shoulders, move your hands outward beyond elbow width. To develop

your upper-back muscles, use the wide grip and pull up, but at the top of the pull place your head in front of the bar.

This all sounds easy, and it no doubt will work, but what if you can't do the first pull-up? There is a solution used by the never-say-die drill instructor. He picked up the recruit and placed him on the pull-up bar with his chin above the bar. Then the recruit slowly lowered his weak, puny, sissy body downward while the DI screamed phrases not printable here. You can use a stool or bench to gain the height needed to place your chin above the bar and then slowly lower your body down. In time, this begins to work if repeated over and over. In boot camp it worked in about thirty days. Even without the inspirational encouragement offered by the military drill instructor, you too will show progress in thirty days. Do these inverse chin-ups as many times a week as possible and with as many repetitions as time permits.

Now let's go back down the body past the tummy to the legs. Walk-ing and jogging have probably already made your legs stronger, but additional exercises will hurry the process along.

Squats without weights can be the beginning. Your upper-body weight will be used to make your legs stronger if the exercise is done properly. Find a pole or a piece of furniture to use as a steadying device or grip. Hold the pole with one hand extended from your shoulder. Now spread your feet to shoulder width. Stand erect and, without bending your back or neck, let your knees slowly bend until the upper parts of your legs (thighs) are parallel to the floor, then, using your leg muscles slowly push back upright to the erect position. At the bottom (squatting position) of this exercise, your knees should be forward of your toes, then when you return to the upright position, your knees are brought back above your toes. Do as many sets of this exercise as you can, rest, and then do more. The primary muscle used in this exercise is your front thigh muscle (quadriceps) although secondary squats use your ham-string muscles and lower-back muscles, as well as the *gluteus maximus*, your butt muscle. Serious weight trainers often rate squats as the single most important exercise they do because it uses so many large muscles. Using only the weight of your upper body, you will notice the effect after sufficient repetitions.

The bench-step or step-up is another method of strengthening your thigh muscles. Find a well-secured step or stool about twelve inches high. Place one foot on the step or stool, and then lift your other foot and place it beside your starting foot on the step. Next lower the foot just placed on the step back to the floor. Do not switch legs until you have exhausted the muscles in the starting leg. Then

switch and repeat the exercise for the other leg. Rest and then repeat the entire procedure.

Walking or running up and down indoor stairs or stadium steps is a superb supplemental workout for your legs and your cardiorespiratory system. Walking up steps uses the same front thigh muscle (quadriceps) as the bench step-ups and also uses the lower calf muscle. When walking up steps, try taking two steps at a time. When running, use every step and try to push off on the ball of your foot. Once

the top is reached, catch your breath and walk down. There is no reason to run back down; that causes too much stress on your knees and ankles. A few round trips of even a small stadium will cause a burning sensation in your quadriceps, and at the top you should be gasping for breath. Welcome to the club. You are out and about doing physical things, and you are not in front of the TV.

If you opt to conduct your strength training at home and not at a gym, these few exercises can be a beginning point. There have been numerous books written on this subject; in time you may want to visit a bookstore and find one.

PHYSICAL ACTIVITY SUMMARY

In the previous section, Structuring Your Program, I attempted to convey a few thoughts on how to start and maintain a program using the most popular forms of physical activity—walking, walking/jogging, running, swimming, cycling, and strength training. These six forms of exercise are the most widely used, but certainly there are others from which to choose and some may be even more enjoyable or more convenient for you. Below I list others aerobic forms with which I am familiar—familiar meaning that I have seen them done, but I have not recently tried to do them.

Cross-training is a term used by coaches and trainers when one participates in more than one form of physical activity. Cross-training is often recommended by these professionals because it is now believed that exercising all muscle groups to build strength and endurance is considerably more beneficial than using only one group of muscles. An example of working only one muscle group is cycling, which obviously uses primarily the legs, thus neglecting the upper body. In professional athletics, cross-training is used to avoid injury because all muscle groups become stronger and more flexible. If cross-training is good enough for the pros, you and I may as well do it, too.

Other forms of activity may fit your needs. You can try aerobic dancing, bench aerobics, water aerobics, roller skating, roller blading, ice skating, cross-country skiing, rowing, jumping rope, stationary cycling, stationary rowing, stair-climbing machines, or stationary skiing.

Any aerobic activities you choose must have the potential to elevate your heart rate and maintain it at the elevated rate for at least twenty continuous minutes, then longer when your endurance level permits. Your chosen aerobic activities combined with strength training will have the therapeutic effect you desire.

When you are out and about running, walking, cycling, or doing other outdoor activities, be sure to take advantage of the pleasant things around you. Even search out these pleasant new experiences. I believe these experiences to be a part of my treatment and hopefully also of yours.

One such experience has brought so many laughs and chuckles that I want to encourage you to follow my path. It is likely that when you are out on the jogging path or the walking and biking route, you will encounter a sidewalk or roadside stand manned by youngsters who are trying to sell something. Normally, the product offered for sale by these youngsters is either lemonade or soft drinks. Keep change with you, always stop, buy something, and strike up a conversation.

One late afternoon while jogging, I approached two four- or five-year-old boys sitting behind a red wagon parked on the sidewalk. The wagon contained three plastic cups, two of which appeared to contain loose gravel. The third cup was empty. After I stopped, the spokesman for the two asked if I wanted to buy a polished rock. I replied, "Maybe. How much are they and how have you boys done?"

"Not much good," replied the spokesman, "We have all of our dime ones left and we sold just one nickel rock." I then pointed to the empty cup and asked if they had sold all of the penny rocks, assuming that the empty cup must have contained the cheaper merchandise and that it had sold out first. "No," explained the little red-headed boy, not the original spokesman, "Those were our for-free rocks and we sold all of them this morning."

I still have a full cup of ten-cent polished rocks and a cup of five-cent rocks minus one. If I need a chuckle, I can always open my desk drawer and see my two cups of polished rocks. When I think back on my bout with depression, it is easy to remember the time that the red-head's comment, "We sold all the for-free ones this morning," would not have amused me. Back then, in the "black dog" days, it is doubtful that I would even have met the two junior merchants because I was never out and about and so little was amusing.

Physical activity washes away the black dog of depression. You are the only one who can administer this simple prescription. You must give it a try.

Do negative thoughts cause depression or is depression the cause of negative thinking? The answer is not known. What is known is the fact that people suffering from depression score higher on the negative portion of thought pattern tests that contain both positive and negative solutions related to the same subject.

Changing your thoughts from destructive thinking to constructive thinking will help you recover from depression. It is believed by some in the mental health field that learning a positive self-communication method can actually prevent the onset of depression in many potential cases. Cognitive therapy is the term used to describe the relearning process. Cognitive therapy is successfully used to treat clinically depressed patients and recently was tested as a treatment method for people who have high levels of depressive symptoms but who do not meet the criteria for diagnosis as clinically depressed.

Cognitive, when used in the context of mental health, means how one perceives his/her own ability and circumstances. In depressed people, the therapy attempts to convert their negative self-perception into a positive self-perception by changing the way they think. Thoughts are sentences we tell ourselves. They are our internal environment. We can learn to change the sentences we speak to ourselves from negative to positive. Yes, you can teach an old dog new tricks!

Your exercise period is a perfect time to learn new ways to talk to yourself. A few guidelines may be helpful, but common sense will be your best instructor.

If you choose to use your exercise periods to practice positive thinking, use the middle period. If you are walking, running, cycling, or swimming, it is difficult to do much heavy thinking once the finish line is close or in view. Often, in the middle of a run, walk, or cycling trip, it is actually helpful to have thoughts other than just those concerning your physical activity. With other thoughts, time passes faster and your pace becomes more relaxed. It is actually difficult to think negatively when engaged in strenuous physical activity, so the time ought to be used to learn positive ways of thinking, which will then be easily transferred to time not spent exercising.

Thoughts—the sentences we tell ourselves—affect our moods, so first learn to recognize the different types of thoughts. "Nothing will ever turn out right for me" is a perfect example of destructive thinking, and the effect is to pull you down. Think constructively: "I'm out here jogging and sweating, so things are changing." You always feel better when you speak a constructive sentence to yourself.

Necessary and unnecessary thoughts occur to all of us. "I must put gas in the car" is a necessary thought for all drivers. "I bet the attendant will damage my car if he checks the oil" is an unnecessary and negative thought. You have not yet asked that the attendant check the oil, and the automobile probably won't be damaged during an oil check.

Positive *versus* negative thinking. Positive thoughts help you feel better. "Things are rough right now, but I'm trying something new to change my life." This thought gives you a good feeling because you are taking action to change your circumstances. If you want to feel worse, say to yourself, "It's no use to try."

Other thought errors can exist when you are depressed. See if any of these are familiar to you. You exaggerate problems and the possible harm they could cause and underestimate your ability to deal with them. You think of a generalization that emphasizes the negative, such as "Nobody likes me." You are impressed by and remember only negative events and usually ignore the positive. You believe that negative things are more likely to happen than are positive things. You think that negative things that happen are always and entirely your fault. You think that positive things that happen either are just luck or should be attributed to someone else. Were a television sports announcer to introduce these thoughts as members of a team, their names would be Exaggerating, Overgeneralizing, Ignoring the Positive, Being Pessimistic and Blaming Oneself—and the largest team member, weighing in at three hundred pounds, is Not Giving Oneself Credit.

When you engage in physical activity, a side effect will be that you will develop a set of tools—new thoughts—that can be used to restructure your thinking when you are not exercising. These tools will be uniquely yours, and they are as valuable as any of your other possessions. Learn to recognize them and use them properly.

It is not necessary to be an accomplished athlete to develop this new vocabulary. These new positive sentences that you say to yourself will develop from the first day you walk and continue to develop as you continue your program. Your first positive thought might be "I did it, I started!" Your phrases will be yours. Mine are "Good, very good!" "I finished!" "Not bad for an old dude." "I tried." "I made it!" "Better next time." " I did it! I did it!" "Good time for me." "Thought I couldn't make it, but I did." "Didn't make it—gotta try again." "I shall be able to do this." "That's my first try." "Not bad, not bad!" Of the dozen or so sentences I often speak to myself there is not one negative thought. These thoughts were learned and stored while engaged in physical activity. The theory that it is difficult, if not impossible, to think negatively when physically active certainly holds true for me.

With this new set of tools—the positive phrases you speak to yourself—you can begin to take constructive action to control your feelings, moods, and other thoughts. When you feel down, depressed, or locked into a hopeless situation, simply telling yourself to feel better has little effect. Combining positive thoughts and positive actions will have the desired positive effect on the way you feel. When you begin a physical activity program, you will have already taken one important positive action. Other pleasant results are often the result of a prolonged physical activity program, and throughout this book these pleasant actions have been mentioned. You meet new and interesting people. You join clubs. You participate in classes. You enter organized events. You plan. You organize. You learn. Positive actions will change your mood for the better. You and only you can identify other positive actions that need to be undertaken in your life situation. Exercise acts as the dress rehearsal for undertaking these additional positive actions and activities. Give something new a try. It will probably work on the first try.

Remember, the fewer pleasant activities you do, the more depressed you will feel. Make a short list of pleasant activities you would like to do in the next two weeks. They need not be expensive activities. When you complete one, add another at the bottom of the list.

Most of us go for days, weeks, and sometimes months without outside recognition of our efforts or our accomplishments. It is not that others are cruel or that they believe we do not contribute—it is simply the way the world works. Little compliments and words of recognition are useful components for a better mental outlook. Would it not seem normal that a new walker might mutter aloud, "Very good, very good," after the first three-mile walk? Why not then use the same phrase after a day's work? When a project really goes haywire and has to be started again, remember the phrase "That's my first try." When the project is finally completed, the phrase "Not bad, not bad" seems to fit nicely. When something is completed and you are not entirely satisfied with the results, which is often the case in physical activity, the thought "Better next time" is healthier than "Well, I messed that up, too."

Here I have told you my dozen one-liners, the sentences I say to myself, and described how I transfer them from a physical activity setting to everyday situations. You will learn your own one-liners and discover how to use them effectively in your life.

If people suffering from depression are to embark on a physical activity program, genuine support from their loved ones and friends will be a great benefit. Depression saps both the energy and the determination to undertake any new activity, let alone an exercise program. Therefore, a great deal of determination will be required of the depressed person.

Support, but do not lead.

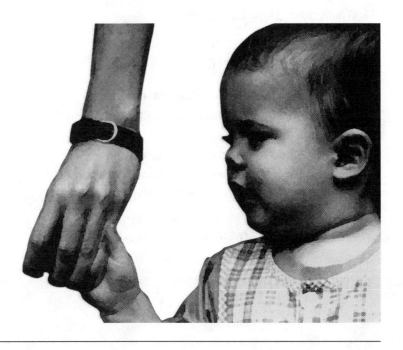

As a family member, spouse, or friend of a person suffering from depression, you should read *Overcoming Depression* by Demitri F. Papolos, MD, and Janice Papolos. This book, published by Harper-Perennial, explains depression and its current treatments in nontechnical terms. The first chapter, titled "The Personal Experience," relates the hopeless, helpless, confused, dull-gray mental make-up and attitude facing people who suffer from unipolar depression. Bipolar depression, or manic-depressive disorder, is also expertly described by Dr. Papolos. Please order this book from your bookstore or the publisher; it is *must* reading for those making up the support group. Every chapter contains much-needed and valuable information. The following table of contents, reprinted from *Overcoming Depression*, reflects the subjects covered by Demitri and Janice Papolos.

FOUR
COMING FULL CIRCLE

Do not assume that most people suffering from depression are of my vintage, which is half a century plus a few years. This mental disorder knows no age bounds. Preteens and teenagers are as likely to suffer as are young adults and those closer to the century mark.

There will be some people suffering from unipolar depression who absolutely cannot embark on a physical activity program until some progress is made through accurate diagnosis and proper medical treatment. Dr. Papolos states that only one in three people suffering from a major mood disorder seeks help and then only one in ten seeks help from a psychiatrist trained to diagnose severe psychiatric disorders and treat them medically.

As a member of the support group, your main task is to secure and encourage the proper medical and psychological treatment. If the medical practitioner believes the patient should begin a physical activity program, you can again be supportive. Note the word *supportive*—not driven, not pushy, not obsessed. Your support can take various forms, depending on the needs of the person you are trying to help.

Help to secure and allot the time needed for a physical activity program. It is important that the support group realize early that time is required for any physical activity. Physical activity in this context is a treatment for a disease. Those making up the support group should not think of the time allotted to this treatment as the time that might be allotted to a hobby or entertainment. It is much more important.

Exercise, or workout, partners are often helpful to those beginning a physical activity program. If you are one of the support group and also assume the role of workout partner, do not push, nag, or orchestrate. Although the workouts may be beneficial to you, they are primarily for the mental health of the other person.

If the person suffering from depression has not shared the contents of this book with his/her medical practitioner, it is important that you do. Perhaps the doctor may have ideas, comments, or words of encouragement, or may want to alter other treatment for compatibility with the activity program. It is important that the medical practitioner know about and keep informed about the physical activity program.

Join me now in the battle to defeat depression by taking your first step toward a healthier and happier life!

In an article that appeared in the medical journal *Primary Care*, Charles W. Smith, Jr., MD, professor of family and community medicine and executive associate dean of clinical affairs at the University of Arkansas for Medical Sciences in Little Rock, provided a primer for other physicians who may wish to use an exercise program as one treatment for depression. The article is titled "Exercise—Practical Treatment for the Patient with Depression and Chronic Fatigue."

Dr. Smith opens his article by describing the difficulty that physicians often face when diagnosing depression in patients. It seems few patients enter the doctor's examining room and announce, "Doc, I am suffering from clinical unipolar depression of a severe nature, and I am here to find out what type of antidepressant medication might best work for me until I am able to sort through the underlying problems I believe are causing my depression." Instead, patients later found to be suffering from depression present the general practitioner, or family doctor, with rather nebulous symptoms such as constant fatigue, insomnia, back pain, neck pain, or headaches. The doctor might hear, "I've lost my energy, don't sleep well, and things, work included, just aren't interesting any more." Each of these symptoms could have an underlying medical cause that might require diagnostic testing to determine. Even when the tests uncover no underlying cause, the doctor may be forced to treat the symptoms. He might treat his patient for a viral infection, hypoglycemia, or allergy—any of these being a reasonable assessment of the patient's problem from the information the patient has verbalized. Much of the diagnostic problem faced by the doctor is created by the fact that most people have great trouble talking about a psychological disorder, especially their own psychological disorder. These patients often have strong defenses against accepting the existence of a psychological problem; therefore, they describe only physical symptoms such as fatigue, insomnia, and the like. Unfortunately, such a description skates smoothly around the underlying issue of depression.

This reluctance to admit and verbalize psychological problems is one reason that many cases of depression go untreated. And, of course, left untreated, episodes of depression often recur. In the last ten years, changes in our social and cultural environment have encouraged people to talk openly about their difficult and sensitive medical and social problems. Admitting and openly discussing depression seems like child's play when compared with discussing the medical, family, and social subjects aired daily on TV talk shows and reported in our local newspapers. But some sufferers still see their depression as evidence of personal weakness or failure. They believe that admitting they suffer from depression is tantamount to telling the world that they are not in complete control of their life and all the related life situations.

If you are reluctant to admit that you suspect, know, or feel that depression is the underlying cause of your symptoms, it is time for you to turn over a new leaf. By not communicating these feelings to your medical practitioner, you are making a silly decision and a big mistake. Depression is certainly not evidence of a human failing, a character flaw, a social misdeed, or conduct not acceptable to the human community. Talk honestly, to the best of your ability, with those you believe can help you overcome this debilitating condition.

Dr. Smith mentions those patients who occasionally have feelings of depression and anxiety but who do not meet the criteria for a diagnosis of clinical depression. He concludes that an exercise program will diminish the frequency and severity of these feelings. Of another group of patients, those who feel chronically fatigued and sluggish, but who also are not depressed, Dr. Smith notes that they are "exercise deficient." After medical testing, no underlying physical cause can be found for their fatigue. Members of this group, commonly referred to as couch potatoes, have simply led an inactive lifestyle for too long a time. This constant inactivity can lead to complaints of fatigue, although the couch potatoes themselves may attribute their feelings of fatigue to the aging process or to job-related stress. When no underlying medical cause for the complaints can be found, a physical activity program is usually the solution to their fatigue problems.

Fatigue and anxiety are not words used exclusively by those people trying to communicate feelings about their depression. Sometimes, some other medical problem may cause these symptoms. The medical practitioner has the difficult task of first finding if there is an underlying physical condition or medical cause. If no medical problem is uncovered, the medical practitioner still must answer another question. "Is the patient really suffering from depression?" Open and accurate communication between the patient and doctor remains the best tool for diagnosing depression.

As Dr. Smith points out, the benefits of aerobic exercise are numerous and varied. In his general and metabolic category, he lists increased endurance, increased aerobic capacity, weight loss, increased HDL levels (HDL is high-density lipoprotein—the good kind of cholesterol), decreased sleep requirements, and increased longevity. Among the psychological benefits—the category that most concerns you and me—he includes increased self-esteem, decreased feelings of stress, decreased type-A behavior, and *decreased depression.* Cardiovascular benefits include decreased coronary heart disease, increased myocardial stroke volume (the amount of blood pumped with each pumping contraction of the heart), decreased resting pulse, increased hemoglobin levels (hemoglobin carries oxygen to the tissue, organs, and muscles of the body), and increased total blood volume. Finally, Dr. Smith lists the musculoskeletal benefits: more capillaries (the small structures that carry blood from the arteries to the rest of the body) and increased muscle volume.

In the remainder of his article, Dr. Smith advises medical practitioners on the ways and means of prescribing and monitoring a physical activity program for patients who are suffering from anxiety and unipolar depression.

Lagniappe, pronounced "lan-yap," is a Creole or Cajun word widely used in southern Louisiana. Lagniappe means a little something extra for no additional charge. The extra might be as small as an extra serving of rice with the blue-plate special or thirteen oysters on the half-shell when only a dozen were ordered. Lagniappe can also be big. A new road might be built through one's property after a meaningful political contribution, or perhaps your child might be the recipient of a four-year scholarship to Tulane, a fine university in New Orleans. In Louisiana people expect some lagniappe from time to time. It's a way of life. With the exception of decreased stress, increased self-esteem, and decreased depression, the benefits Dr. Smith describes are mostly lagniappe—a little something extra for no extra effort. As they say in bayou country, "Laissez les bons temps rouler"—let the good times roll!

※ ※ ※

In an article published in *Sports Medicine* in 1990, Egil W. Martinsen of the Department of Psychiatry at the Central Hospital of Sognog Fjordane, Forde, Norway, makes several important points:

• Generally, depressed patients are physically sedentary.

• Exercise produces an antidepressant effect in patients with mild to moderate forms of nonbipolar (unipolar) depressive disorders.

• Patients appreciate physical exercise and rank exercise to be the most important element in comprehensive treatment programs.

• Exercise seems to be a promising new approach in the treatment of unipolar depressive disorders of mild to moderate severity.

Dr. Martinsen explains that most experiments have used self-reporting tests such as the Beck Depression Inventory. In one study conducted by the doctor, 235 patients were screened for their physical activity level before admission to Modum Bads Nervesanatorium. The majority of the patients were suffering from unipolar depression, the mean age was thirty-nine, and only twenty-three percent of these patients exercised regularly. A previous national survey in Norway indicated that fifty percent of the same-age population performed regular exercise. This indicates that depressed patients may be physically more sedentary compared with the general population.

Yet another study found that the physical work capacity of ninety depressed subjects was below that of similar individuals of the normal population. The physical exercise portion of this study, which consisted of riding stationary bicycles, showed that the mean physical work capacity was eighty-three percent of that of the normal population. But there was also good news: the lung function of the ninety patients was equal to or exceeded that of members of the general population who were the same age and sex as those participating in the study.

In 1985 and 1987 Dr. Martinsen studied forty-nine hospitalized patients who met the *DSM III* (*Diagnostic and Statistical Manual,* third update) criteria for major depression. While hospitalized, about half of these patients—those in the control group—attended one or two sessions of psychotherapy and three sessions of occupational therapy each week. The remaining half—the exercise or experimental group—substituted one hour of aerobic workout for each of the three occupational therapy sessions. Nine people in the exercise training group and fourteen people in the control group received tricyclic antidepressant medication. The level of depression was assessed by the Beck Depression Inventory test and by therapist rating using the Comprehensive Psychopathological Rating Scale. After six weeks and nine weeks, there was a significant increase in the physical work capacity (PWC) of the aerobic group; the control group, however, was unchanged in PWC from pretest scores. Both groups (control and exercise) showed reduction in depression scores, but the reduction in the aerobic training group was significantly greater than in the control group. Those patients who were on tricyclic antidepressants had reductions in depression scores similar to those who did not use medication.

In 1989 Dr. Martinsen and associates conducted an experiment designed to compare aerobic and nonaerobic forms of exercise as they relate to the treatment of unipolar depression. Ninety-nine hospitalized patients who met the *DSM III*-R criteria for unipolar depression were assigned either to a walking/running/aerobic group or to a training group for muscular strength, endurance, flexibility, coordination, and relaxation—that is, for weight, strength, and endurance training. The two groups exercised in their assigned groups for one hour three times per week for eight weeks. In testing, the aerobic group showed a significant increase in aerobic capacity. The nonaerobic group was unchanged as to heart and lung capability. Each group, however, showed a similar reduction in depression scores. In each group fourteen patients were administered tricyclic antidepressant medication. Although twenty-eight patients using antidepressant medication had a somewhat larger reduction in depression scores than those who did not use medication, according to Dr. Martinsen and staff the difference was not statistically significant.

Depressed people have a tendency to be physically out of shape. Physical activity at least three times a week helps alleviate unipolar depression with or without the assistance of antidepressant medication. Those taking antidepressant medication also benefit from physical activity. Both strength training (weightlifting) and aerobics (walking/running) do the trick. Why not do both?

Dr. Martinsen noted, "Depressive disorders have a great tendency for relapse. The value of self-administered strategies such as exercise is therefore highly dependent on the degree to which the patients continue with the activity after the termination of the training programs." More than half of the patients he studied continued their exercise programs one year after the training period. This 50% rate does not seem to vary greatly from the normal population that started an exercise program twelve months earlier. Without absolute hard statistical evidence to back his statement, the doctor concluded, "Those who continue with regular exercise tend to have lower depression scores than sedentary ones, but the strength of correlation between exercise adherence and depression scores is unclear."

If exercise helps, stay with it. If one form of physical activity gets boring, find another one quickly. Above all, do not be among the fifty percent who quit.

Dr. Martinsen observed that a common attitude among psychiatric and health workers has been that depressed patients do not like to take part in strenuous exercise programs. The good doctor and his associates had the common sense to ask their patients to rank the usefulness of exercise as compared with other forms of treatment. This study showed that patients evaluated physical fitness training as the most important element in the comprehensive treatment program. It ranked above traditional forms of therapy, including psychotherapy, milieu therapy, and medication.

If the patients like it and it works, don't change it.

Dr. Martinsen discussed several explanations for the efficacy of exercise as depression therapy:

• the temporary increase in body temperature that accompanies intensive exercise contributes to a sense of well-being; also, plasma (blood) catecholamine concentrations at a constant exercise intensity have been shown to be lower following endurance training;

• lymphocyte-B receptors activity also increased as a result of aerobic endurance training;

•an increase in circulating B-endorphin concentrations appears to occur with endurance exercise;

• an increase in the concentrations of monoamines in the brain also has been postulated to accompany aerobic exercise.

The good doctor ended by stating, "It is important to note that empirical evidence linking these biological phenomena to depression is still lacking."

Exercise must alter something in the brain chemistry that is not yet fully understood by the scientific community. The researchers will eventually unlock the exact reasons. However, I use a television, radio, computer, light bulb, and microwave even though I haven't a clue as to why they work. If getting hot, sweaty, and out of breath will alleviate depression, I'll also use exercise.

Six doctors at the University of Rochester—Deborah J. Ossip-Klein, Elizabeth J. Doyne, Eric D. Bowman, Kent M. Osborn, Ilona B. McDougall-Wilson, and Robert A. Neimeyer—conducted a two-part study of clinically depressed women. In the first part of their study, they demonstrated that both running and weightlifting produce long-term improvements in depression scores for clinically depressed women and that these results are not dependent on achieving an improved aerobic fitness level. The second part of the study, reported in 1989, dealt with self-concept. Forty women were recruited through mass media ads to participate in a study of the effects of exercise on depression. The women had to meet the following conditions and standards:

• be 18 to 35 years old;

• meet research diagnostic criteria (RDC) for major or minor depressive disorder;

• agree to all experimental conditions;

• agree not to receive other treatment for depression or engage in any nonprescribed exercise program;

• meet requirement of no hospitalization for depression within the past year;

• show no evidence of manic-depressive disorder, suicide threat, or physical contraindications to exercise.

After the initial study, thirty-two women completed all follow-up assessments. These thirty-two had reported a mean of 4.55 previous episodes of depression. Originally, the forty were assigned to one of three groups: a delayed treatment or control group, a running group, or a weightlifting group. Subjects in the two activity groups exercised individually in a sports facility at the University of Rochester under the supervision of trained undergraduate monitors. Monitors were rotated to minimize the possible effects of continuing supportive contact with a particular monitor.

For eight weeks the subjects attended four exercise sessions per week. The runners/walkers used a one-eighth-mile track and ran or walked for twenty minutes. Their heart rate was monitored at seven-minute intervals to ensure that a target rate of eighty percent of the estimated maximum work capacity would be maintained.

Subjects in the weightlifting group went through a twenty-minute, ten-station program using Universal Machines. Their heart rate was monitored to ensure that it stayed within the nonaerobic range. The control group did nothing for the eight weeks of the study but were then offered an opportunity to participate in either of the two activity programs.

All groups were tested before, during, and after treatment. The two exercise groups were also tested one, seven, and twelve months after the exercise treatments. In this second experiment, self-concept was measured using two tests, the Beck Self-Concept Test and Osgood's Semantic Differential. Beck consists of twenty-five adjectives on which the subjects use a five-point scale to rate themselves in relation to others. Osgood's Semantic Differential consists of fourteen seven-point scales, anchored on either end, with opposite adjectives relevant to self-concept and fitness.

Using the Beck Self-Concept Test, the pretreatment mean score for the track exercise group was 72.8, that of the weightlifting group was 73.25, and that of the control group, was 74.38. These score levels indicate low self-concept on the part of all three groups that participated in the experiment. Eight weeks later, after attending only four exercise sessions per week, the mean score for the track-exercise group had improved to 80.90, the weightlifting group had improved to 79.58, but the control group had declined to 73.00. This is a significant improvement for both runners and weightlifters. To further substantiate the results of improved self-concept brought about by physical activity, the Osgood Semantic Differential Test was administered both before and after treatment. The pretreatment mean scores obtained on the Osgood Test were 44.27 for runners, 45.71 for weightlifters, and 45.09 for the control group. On completion of the test, the mean scores were 65.64, 68.00, and 52.27, respectively.

Eight weeks are a tiny investment of time to acquire a better attitude toward yourself. A better self-image may be only a side effect of physical activity, but what a pleasant side effect it is! Members of the control group, who did not exercise during this two-month period, were not blessed with a better attitude toward themselves.

The results of the present study indicate that exercise enhanced self-concept in a population of clinically depressed women. Both track and weightlifting groups showed significantly improved self-concept relative to the control group, and the effects persisted over time. In general, no differences were found between exercise groups; where differences did occur, they slightly favored the weightlifting group.

An abbreviated table from this experiment, Table 1, is printed later in the appendix. It tabulates the results discussed above and shows how the improved self-image lasted over time. The same self-concept tests were administered after completion of the treatment at one-, seven-, and twelve-month intervals. You may find this additional information of interest.

In an article titled "Effects of Aerobic and Nonaerobic Exercise on Depression and Self-Concept" by Paula N. Stein and Robert W. Motta of the Hofstra University in Hempstead, New York, published in *Perceptual and Motor Skills* in 1992, the authors examine and comment on a host of previous studies of the effects of exercise on depression. They cite a study published in 1987 in which seventy-five males, judged to exemplify a type-A personality, were assigned to either an aerobic exercise conditioning class or a nonaerobic weight-training control group. Analysis indicated that although the weight-training group did not enhance aerobic functioning, significantly decreased levels of depression as measured by the Beck Depression Inventory and the Symptom Check List-90 were reported. The study concluded that whereas both aerobic exercise and nonaerobic training equally relieve self-reported depression, the improvements were not associated with the change in cardiovascular conditioning *per se.*

For their study, Stein and Motta selected eighty-nine college students attending a private university in Nassau County, New York. Their average age was twenty years, and for inclusion the subjects were required not to have had training in aerobic or nonaerobic exercise for at least three months before the initiation of the experiment. The students were divided into three groups: weight training, swim for fitness, and control. The control group, or classroom group, had to refrain from any exercise during the study. The two exercise classes met for ninety minutes twice weekly for seven weeks. The swim group performed Cooper's Twelve-Minute Swim during the first and last class sessions to assess changes in cardiac efficiency and aerobic conditioning. Cooper's Swim, which counts the number of laps a person can swim continuously in twelve minutes, is considered to be a reliable measure of aerobic improvement. It was intended that the swimmers improve their aerobic conditioning, so they were taught to keep their heart rate between 70% and 85% of the maximum rate for at least twenty minutes during their training period. The maximum heart rate is 220 beats per minute minus age in years. The average age of this group was twenty. Thus, $220 - 20 = 200 \times 70\% = 140$ beats per minute minimum, or $200 \times 85\% = 170$ beats per minute maximum. The maximum rate to which a twenty-year-old should increase his/her heart rate during a twenty-minute workout is 170. As age increases, the maximum beats per minute decreases.

The swimming group was measured and tested for mood change and self-concept, and improvements in aerobic fitness were tested using the lap number recorded during Cooper's Twelve-Minute Swim. The nonaerobic exercise (weightlifting) group engaged in progressive resistance training exercises (PREs) using both free weights and Universal machines. The goals were to improve muscle strength by low repetitions at high resistance and muscle endurance by high repetitions at low resistance. Members of the control group were enrolled in an introductory college-level course in psychology.

Using the Depression Adjective Check List and the Beck Depression Inventory as testing tools, Stein and Motta found that the aerobic and nonaerobic groups experienced greater decreases in depression than did the control group. The Tennessee Self-Concept Scale detected significant differences between the two exercise groups. The nonaerobic (weightlifting) group exhibited a higher overall self-concept than did either the aerobic (swimming) group or the control (classroom) groups.

This study again demonstrates that both aerobic activity and weightlifting have a positive mood-changing effect on those suffering from depression. Weightlifting has the added value of improving one's self-concept. Why not combine the two? You definitely should.

※ ※ ※

Swimmers Really Do Feel Better! Although two of my children were competitive swimmers from about age eight, I was not aware that swimmers felt better than the normal nonswimming population. All I remember is that as teenagers they ate more than any other member of the normal adult population. In the peak training season, they would sometimes swim 15,000 yards in a two-sessions-a-day workout. Remembering, I really believe they each required one calorie per yard per day.

In the October 1983 issue of *Psychosomatic Medicine*, Bonnie Berger and David Owen reported a study of the effects of swimming on normal-mood college students, male and female, ranging in age from seventeen to fifty years. They cite recent evidence that suggests that moderately strenuous jogging produces a variety of desirable psychological changes that support runners' claims of reduced anxiety and depression and that running also seems to enhance one's self-concept, self-esteem, self-awareness, vigor, and clear-mindedness. These desirable changes have encouraged psychotherapists to recommend running to clients who are clinically anxious or depressed. In view of the psychological benefits of jogging, it is surprising that the effects of other forms of recreational exercise have not been investigated. Such a study is important because of the large number of individuals for whom other forms of exercise are physically difficult or impossible but who might emotionally as well as physically benefit from an exercise program. Thus, therapists who prescribe running or jogging could present their clients with an additional choice.

Berger and Owen hypothesized that members of the experimental group (swimmers) would report greater mood changes when tested before and after exercise than would members of a control group who were tested before and after a lecture class, that the effects on mood would be similar to those reported for running, and that mood changes would differ in degree for men and women swimmers but that the changes would be in the same direction.

Two self-administered tests, the Profile of Mood Survey and the Lie Scale of the Eysenek Personality Inventory, were used to measure mood changes in these normal, nondepressed, students.

As happens in most studies and experiments, all the ingredients were in place: the hypotheses were identified, the volunteer students were selected, the classroom instructors were available for the control group, the swimming pool was available, and the testing mechanism was reliable. The only problem was that some of these subjects could not swim. Some could not swim seventy-five feet, let alone swim for forty minutes. The only solution was to teach them to swim. Thus, the study consisted of a beginner's class of swimmers (those unable to swim seventy-five feet), an intermediate class (those able to swim seventy-five feet or more), and a control group of classroom students. The swimmers met and were taught twice a week in forty-minute sessions for a fourteen-week fall semester. The control group met three times a week for fifty minutes in class sessions. All students were informed of the purpose of the study and the testing that would be required.

In earlier studies, individuals who scored near the mean on mood scales had not shown reliable mood changes as a result of exercise. However, the swimmers in this study initially earned scores within the normal range for college students and reported significant positive mood changes after swimming. Using the two tests mentioned above, it was possible to measure various components of mood in these normal students. The tests measured tension, depression, anger, vigor, fatigue, and confusion for beginning swimmers, male and female, intermediate swimmers, male and female, and finally the control group, male and female. From the outset, scores showed that women were significantly less angry, and possibly less depressed, than men. For both swimming groups, a comparison of the scores obtained before the swim class with those obtained after the class indicated that tension decreased, depression decreased, anger decreased, vigor increased, fatigue was virtually unchanged for the males but decreased for the females, and confusion decreased for both male and female students.

The mood testing was conducted after the third month of biweekly instruction, by which time both beginning and intermediate swimmers were likely to have developed sufficient skill to complete twenty minutes of aerobic exercise during the forty-minute class session.

Keep in mind that the participants in this study were mood-normal college students, not people suffering from depression, and they reported feeling even better when they swam. For the depressed person this opens up an entirely new set of activities that can be learned. If you can't swim, learn. If you can't ride a bike, learn. If you can't skate, learn. This quest for new activities and a willingness to learn will allow you to vary your physical activity program and select those activities that are most enjoyable to you. The learning process will also be enjoyable.

The test results of the swimmers' study, Table 2, are printed in abbreviated form on a later page of the appendix.

TABLE 1. Results from Beck Self-Concept Test: *University of Rochester Study*

	Baseline	Before Treatment	During Treatment	After Treatment	After 1 Month	After 7 Months	After 12 Months
Measure							
Track M	73.00	72.80	76.00	80.90	78.90	82.98	81.04
Universal M	75.29	73.25	76.67	79.58	82.50	83.13	78.88
Wait List M	72.36	74.38	72.50	73.00			
Semantic Differential							
Track M	44.70	44.27	58.36	65.64	64.55	59.91	59.39
Universal M	47.40	45.71	65.00	68.00	67.67	71.48	68.98
Wait List M	46.45	45.09	42.79	52.27			

M is 0000000.

TABLE 2. Marginal Statistics for Swimmers: *"Swimmers Feel Better" Study*

	Beginners		Intermediates		Controls	
Months	Male	Female	Male	Female	Male	Female
Measured	14	11	17	16	14	28
Pretest Results						
Tension	45.4	41.2	45.9	44.8	43.1	40.5
Depression	48.4	42.2	46.8	48.4	43.4	42.8
Anger	52.1	42.2	48.5	48.9	45.9	42.0
Vigor	56.9	49.0	48.2	50.9	50.1	48.4
Fatigue	45.4	47.1	46.2	46.2	47.1	42.8
Confusion	46.1	40.6	44.3	44.4	45.1	40.0
Posttest Results						
Tension	41.6	38.5	41.9	38.1	42.4	39.6
Depression	46.3	40.3	44.9	43.2	42.6	41.2
Anger	48.5	40.5	45.5	44.6	46.4	40.7
Vigor	58.9	50.1	48.8	55.5	49.1	47.3
Fatigue	46.0	44.9	45.9	44.2	44.9	44.5
Confusion	42.0	36.2	42.5	39.9	43.9	38.8

Diagnostic Criteria for a Major Depressive Episode

A. At least five of the following symptoms have been present nearly every day during a two-week period and represent a change from previous functioning; at least one of the symptoms is either depressed mood or loss of interest or pleasure.

1. Depressed or irritable mood most of the day.

2. Markedly diminished interest or pleasure in all, or almost all, activities most of the day.

3. Significant weight loss when not dieting or significant weight gain, or decrease or increase in appetite (in children, consider failure to make expected weight gains).

4. Insomnia or hypersomnia (sleeping excessively).

5. Psychomotor agitation or retardation.

6. Fatigue or loss of energy.

7. Feelings of worthlessness or excessive or inappropriate guilt (which may be delusional), not merely self-reproach or guilt about being sick.

8. Diminished ability to think or concentrate, or indecisiveness.

9. Recurrent thoughts of death (not just fear of dying), recurrent suicidal ideation without a specific plan, or a suicide attempt or a specific plan for committing suicide.

B. One or both of the following situations exists.

1. Cannot be established that an organic factor initiated and maintained the disturbance.

2. Disturbance not a normal reaction to the death of a loved one (uncomplicated bereavement).

C. At no time during the disturbance have there been delusions or hallucinations for as long as two weeks in the absence of prominent mood symptoms (i.e., before the mood symptoms developed or after they have remitted).

D. The condition is not superimposed on schizophrenia, schizophreniform disorder, delusional disorder, or psychotic disorder.

Diagnostic Criteria for a Manic Episode

A. The individual experiences a distinct period of abnormally and persistently elevated, expansive, or irritable mood.

B. During the period of mood disturbance, at least three of the following symptoms have persisted (four if the mood is only irritable) and have been present to a significant degree.

1. Inflated self-esteem or grandiosity.

2. Decreased need for sleep, e.g., feels rested after only three hours of sleep.

3. More talkativeness than usual, or pressure to keep talking.

4. Mental disarray, such as flight of ideas or subjective feeling that thoughts are racing.

5. Distractibility, i.e., attention is too easily drawn to unimportant or irrelevant external stimuli.

6. Increased goal-directed activity (socially, at work or school, or sexually) or psychomotor agitation.

7. Excessive involvement in pleasurable activities that have a high potential for painful consequences, e.g., the person engages in unrestrained buying sprees, sexual indiscretions, or foolish business investments.

C. The mood disturbance is sufficiently severe to cause marked impairment of functioning in occupational or usual social activities or relationships with others, or disturbance is severe enough to necessitate hospitalization to prevent harm to self or others.

D. At no time during the disturbance have there been delusions or hallucinations for as long as two weeks in the absence of prominent mood symptoms (i.e., before the mood symptoms developed or after they have remitted).

E. The condition is not superimposed on schizophrenia, schizophreniform disorder, delusional disorder, or psychotic disorder.

F. It cannot be established that an organic factor initiated and maintained the disturbance.

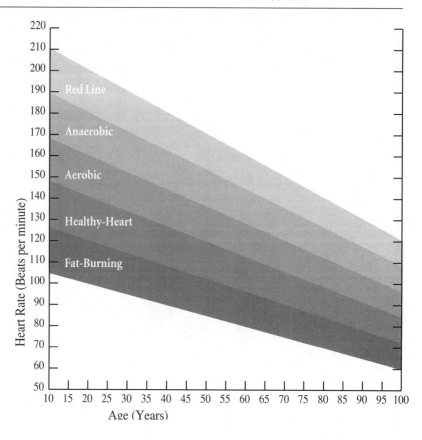

My Week

Dates _____ and _____

My Plan	Monday	Tuesday	Wednesday
M _____ T _____ W _____ T _____ F _____ S _____ S _____			
	M+	M+	M+
Thursday	Friday	Saturday	Sunday
M+	M+	M+	M+

My Week

Dates _____ and _____

My Plan
M _____
T _____
W _____
T _____
F _____
S _____
S _____

Monday		Tuesday		Wednesday	
	M+		M+		M+

Thursday		Friday		Saturday		Sunday	
M+		M+		M+		M+

My Week

Dates _____ and _____

My Plan	Monday	Tuesday	Wednesday
M T W T F S S			
	M+	M+	M+

Thursday	Friday	Saturday	Sunday
M+	M+	M+	M+